Christmas Coloring Book

MAGICAL WINTER HOLIDAYS

Volume 1

Christmas Coloring Books For

Relaxation, Meditation and Creativity

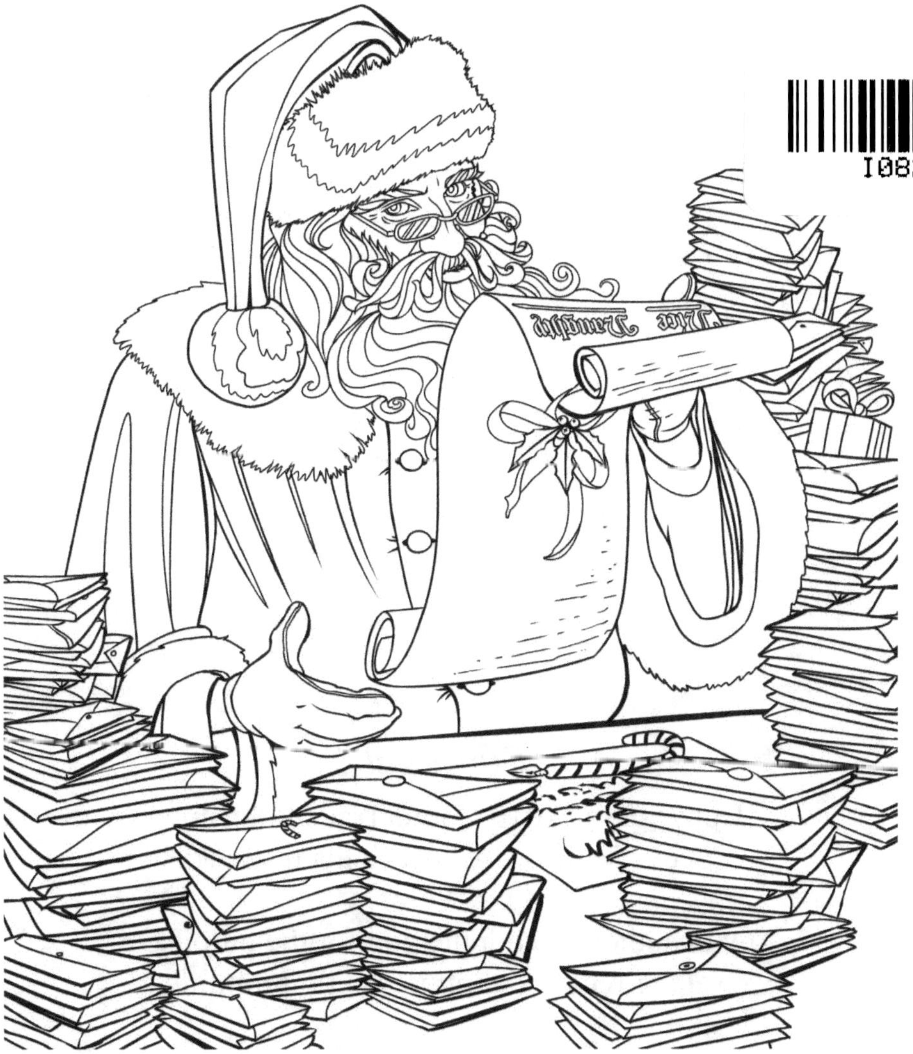

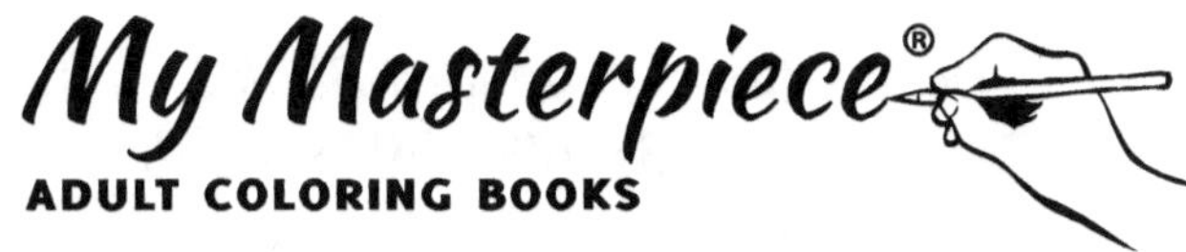

My Masterpiece®

Adult Coloring Books

My Masterpiece® brings you 30 delightful hand-drawn illustrations to whisk you away from the world of busyness and stress and take you to that restful place where you can relax, unwind and have some fun.

BONUS: Included in this book are 10 free Christmas Kaleidoscopes for you to color and enjoy, plus samples from some of our other adult coloring books.

We provide the creative framework and you provide the artistic imagination, using your favorite coloring implements and colors to create your own "Masterpiece".

Each illustration is on its own page so you won't experience bleed-through with colored pencils or gel pens. If you use markers, it is recommended that you place an additional piece of paper behind the illustration you are working on to help protect the next illustration.

We hope you enjoy coloring these wonderful illustrations and creating your very own "My Masterpiece".

Copyright

Illustrations by Daniel J Chamberlin

International Standard Book Number
ISBN 13: 978-0692806258
ISBN 10: 0692806253

Share Your Masterpiece!

Post your colored pages with the hashtag: #MyMasterpieceContest on Instagram, Facebook, Twitter, and Pinterest so we can show off your artistic flair.

Visit www.MyMasterpieceColoring.com to see all the ways you can enter to win great prizes in our monthly Giveaways!

Go To: www.MyMasterpieceColoring.com

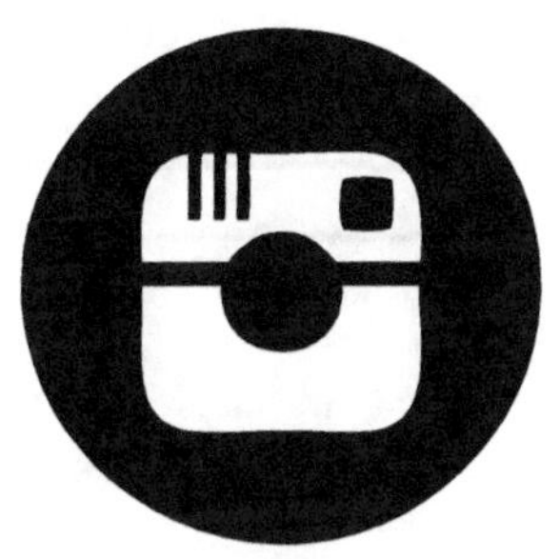

Follow us on Instagram:
www.Instagram.com/MyMasterpieceColoring

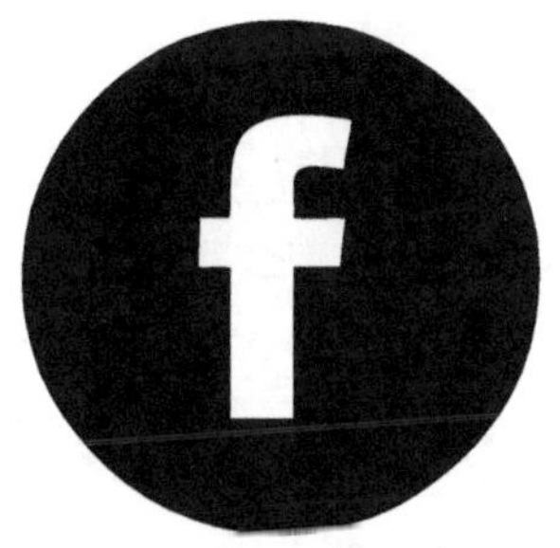

Follow us on Facebook:
www.Facebook.com/MyMasterpieceColoring

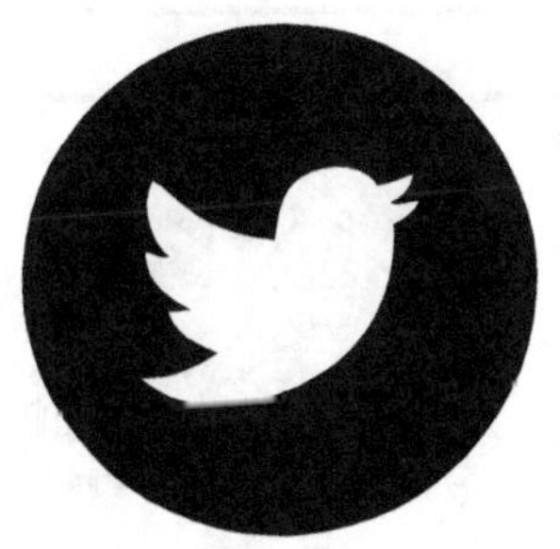

Follow us on Twitter:
www.Twitter.com/MyMasterpieceCo

Follow us on Pinterest:
www.Pinterest.com/MyMasterpieces

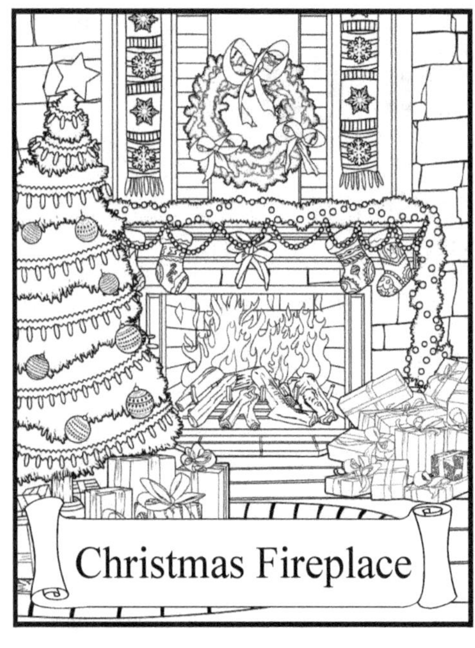

Christmas Fireplace

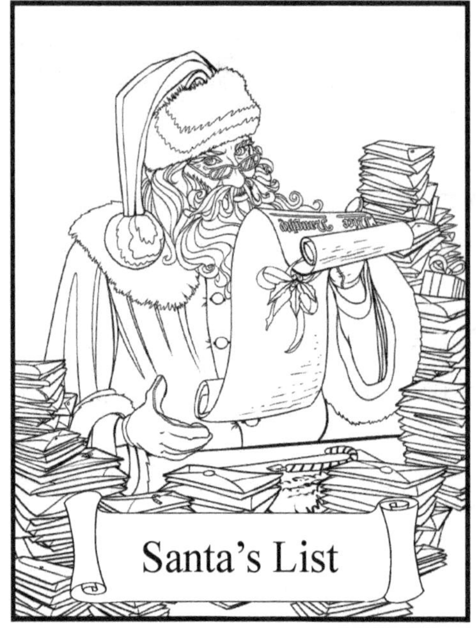

Santa's List

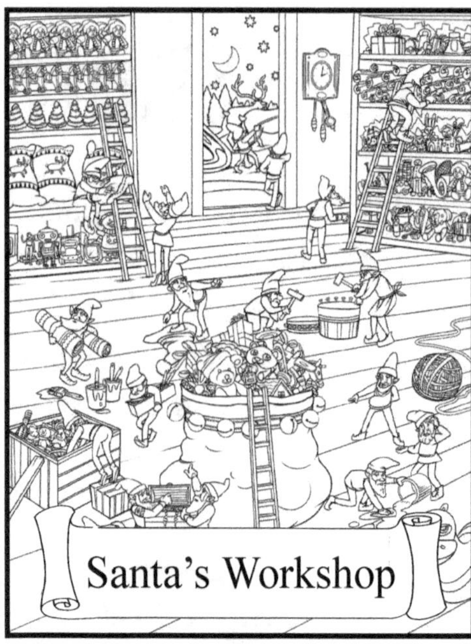

Santa's Workshop

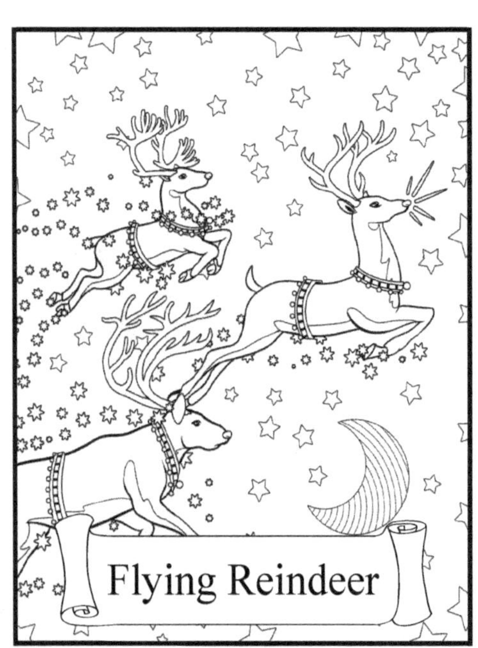

Flying Reindeer

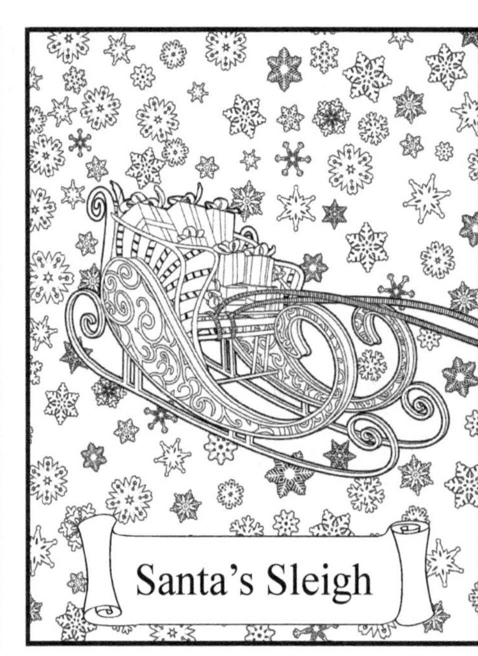

Santa's Sleigh

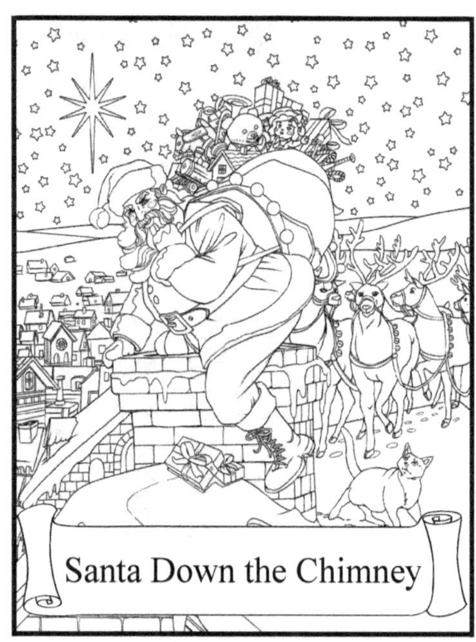

Santa Down the Chimney

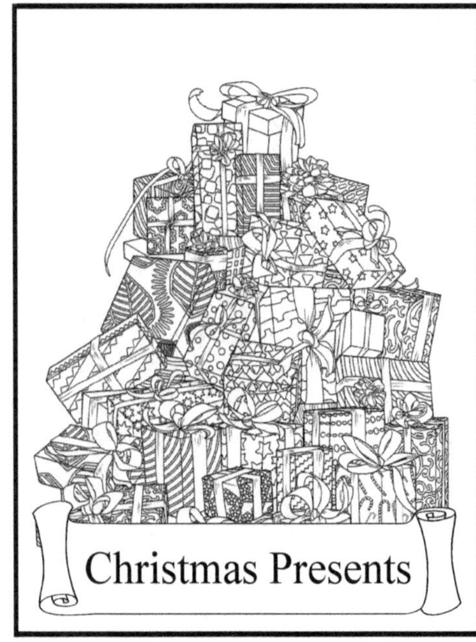

Christmas Presents

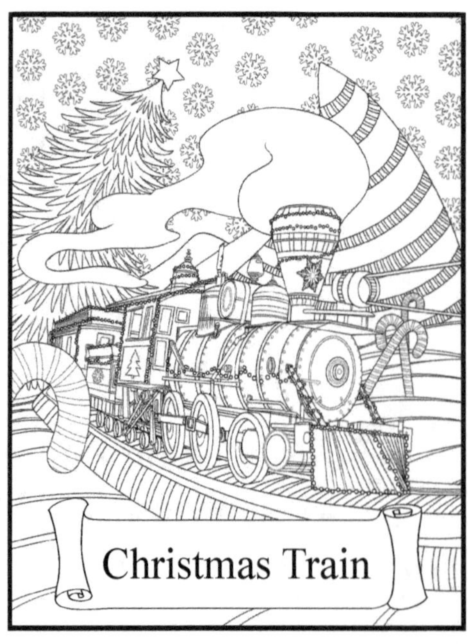

Christmas Train

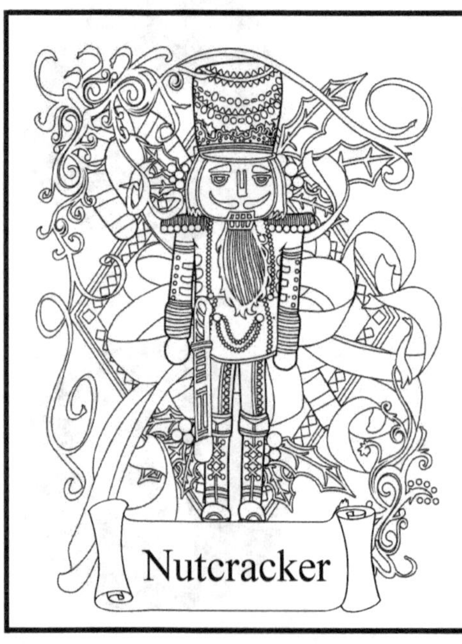

Nutcracker

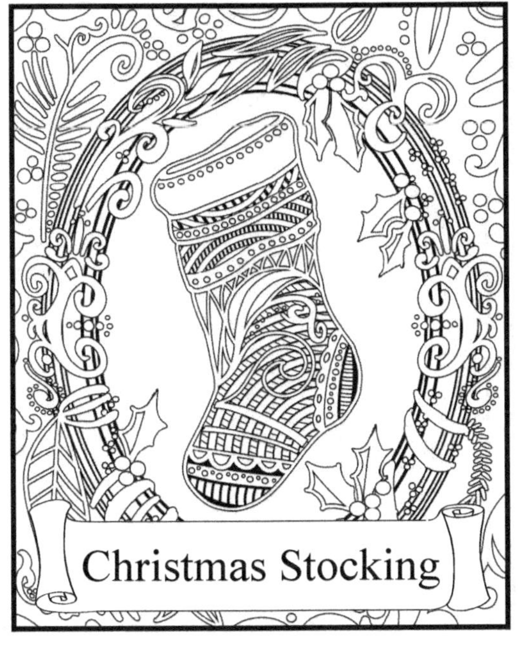
Christmas Stocking

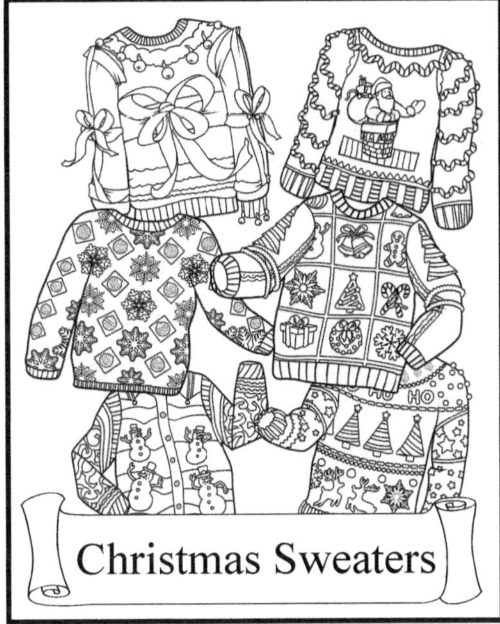
Christmas Sweaters

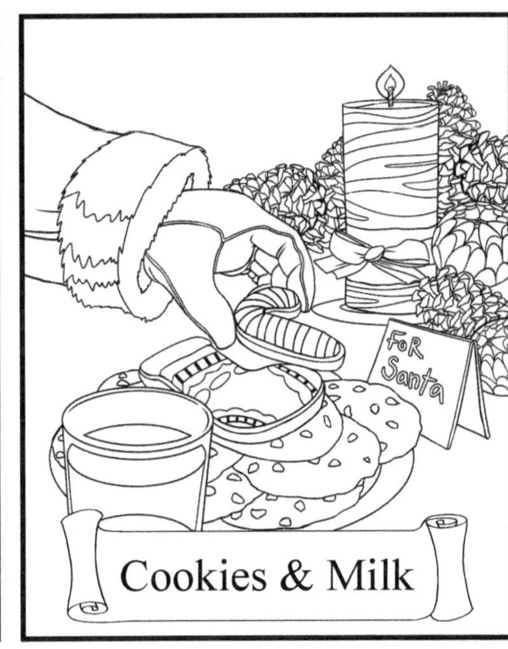
FoR Santa
Cookies & Milk

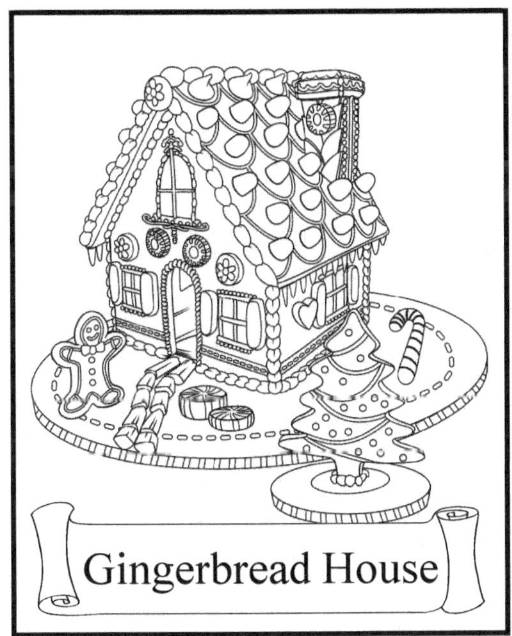
Gingerbread House

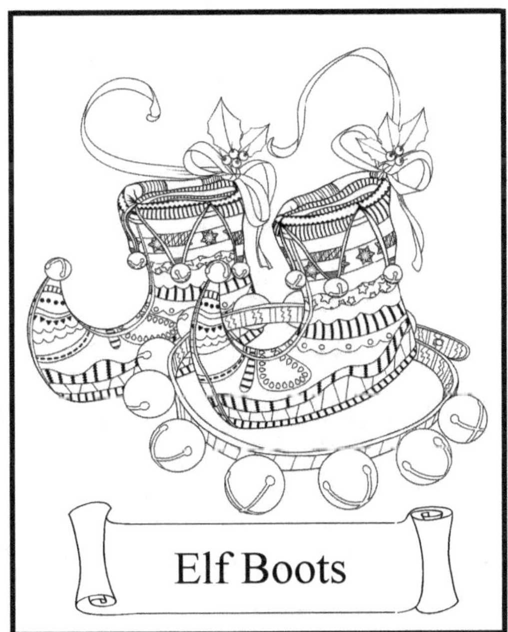
Elf Boots

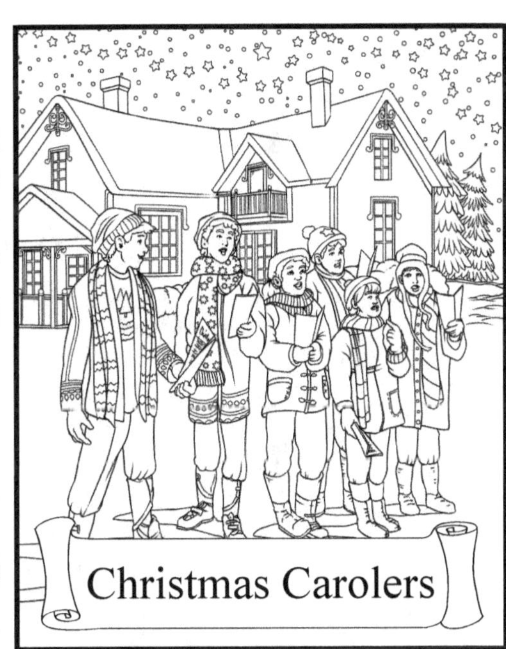
Christmas Carolers

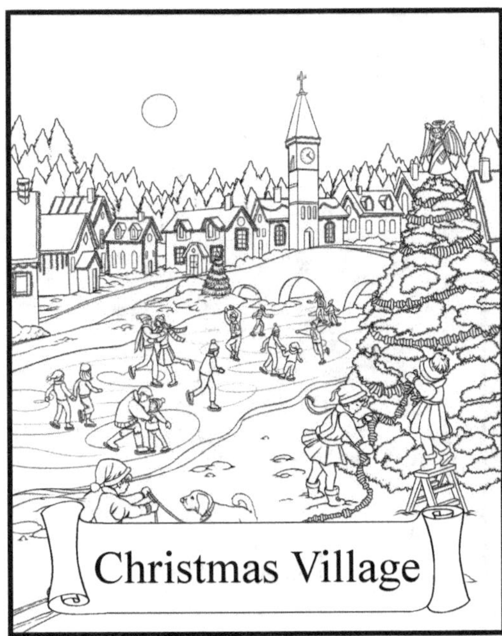
Christmas Village

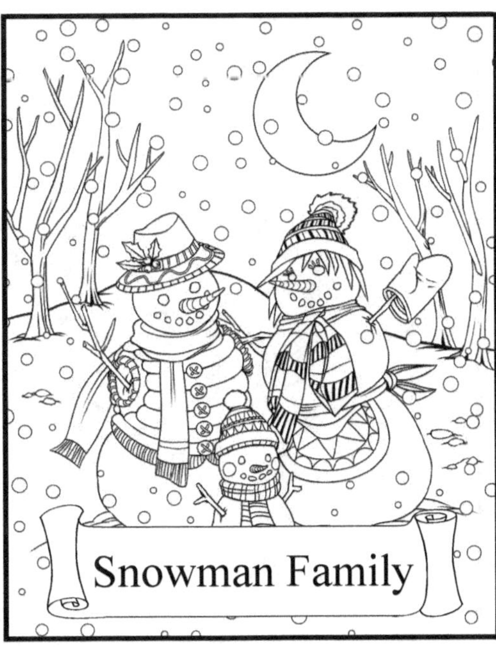
Snowman Family

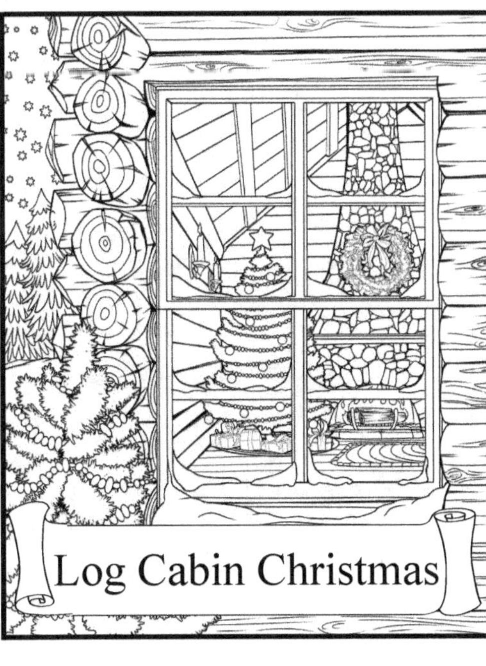
Log Cabin Christmas

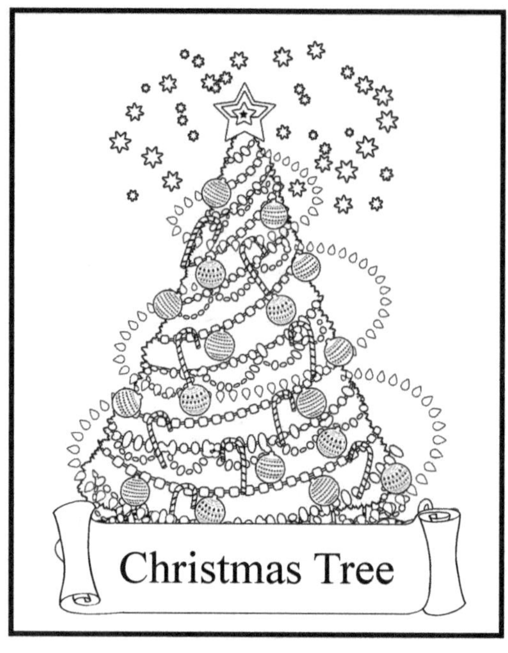
Christmas Tree
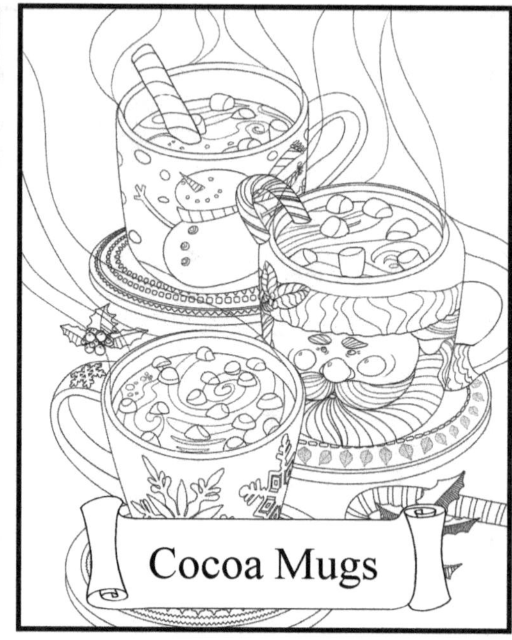
Cocoa Mugs
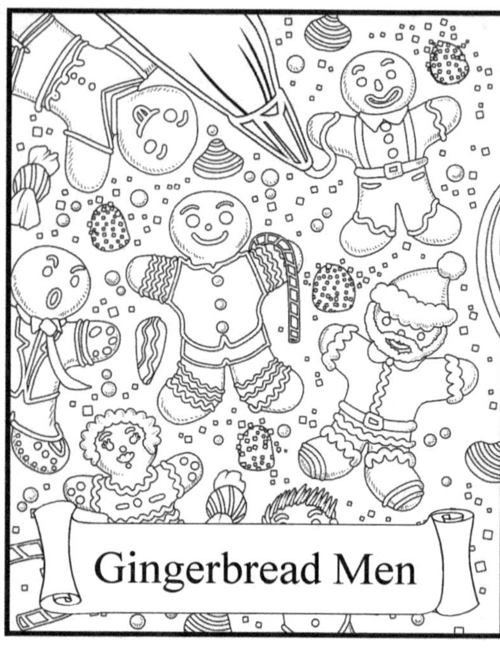
Gingerbread Men
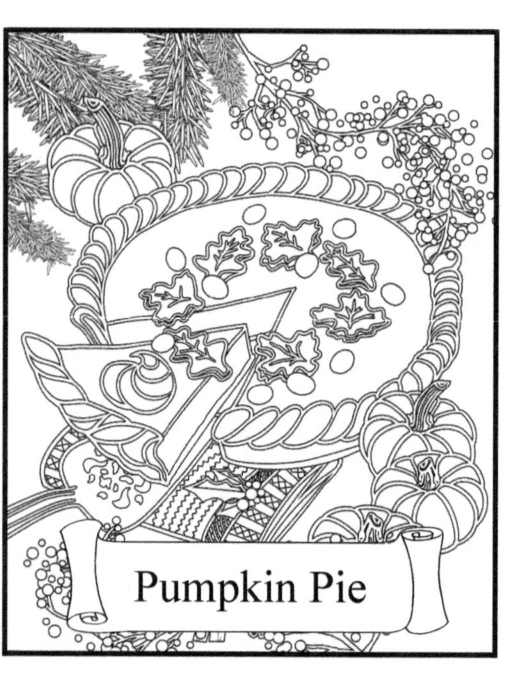
Pumpkin Pie
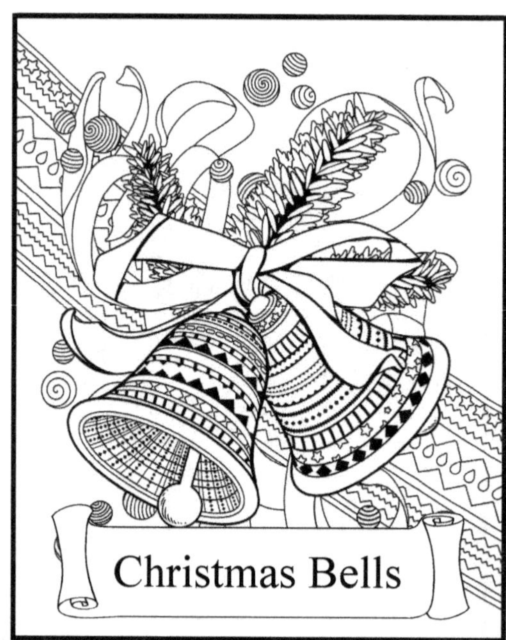
Christmas Bells
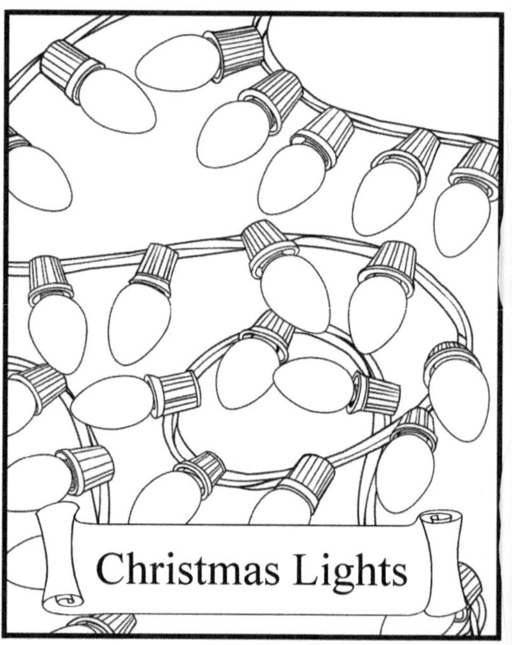
Christmas Lights
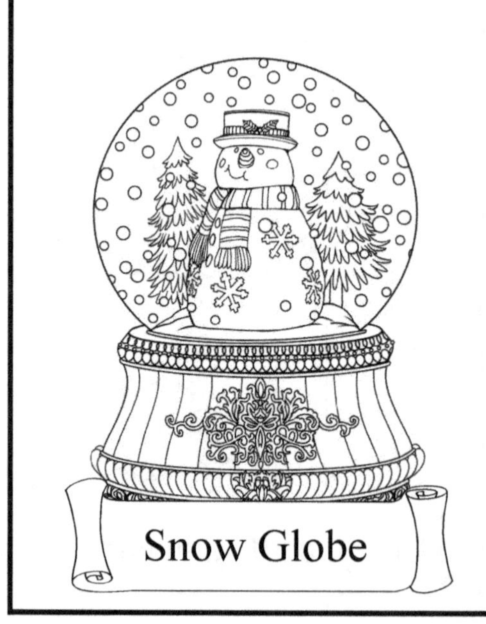
Snow Globe
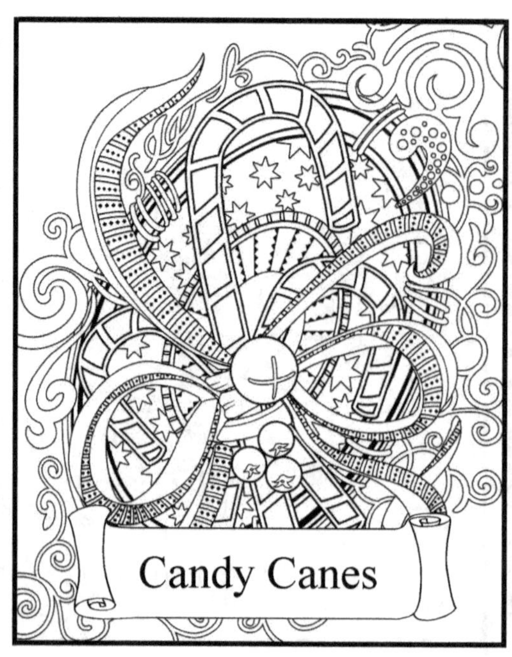
Candy Canes
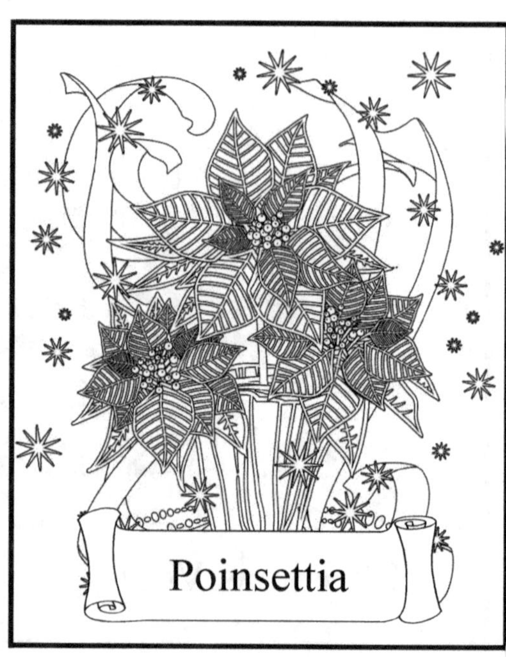
Poinsettia

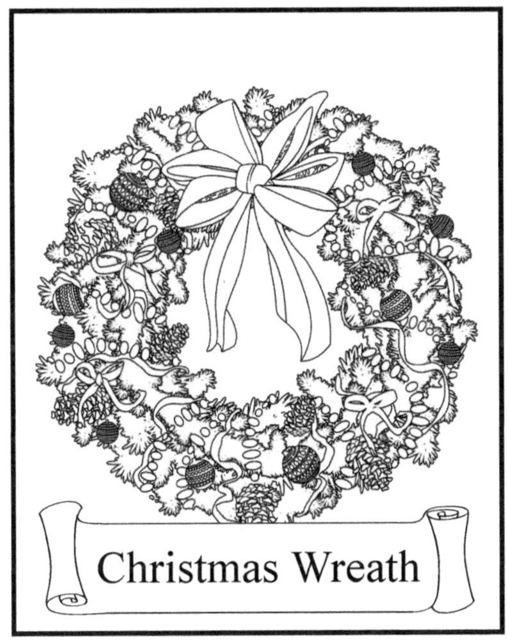
Christmas Wreath

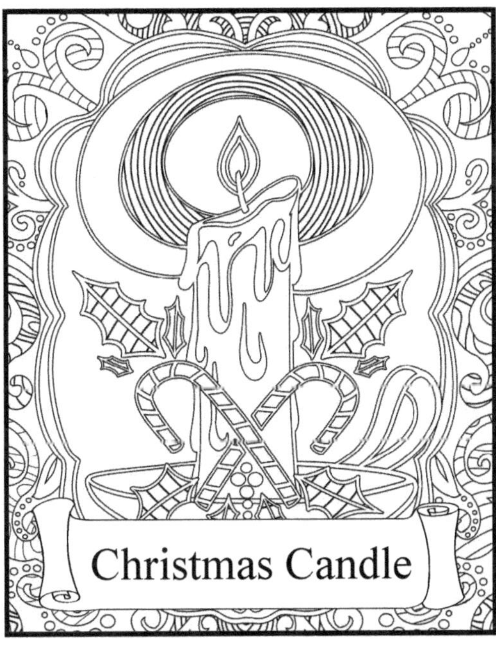
Christmas Candle

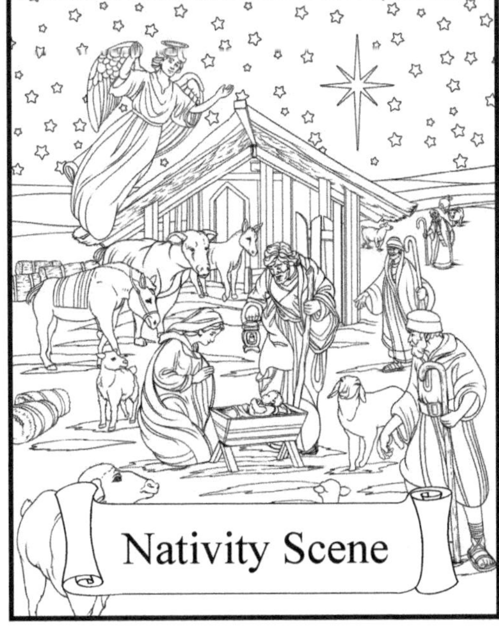
Nativity Scene

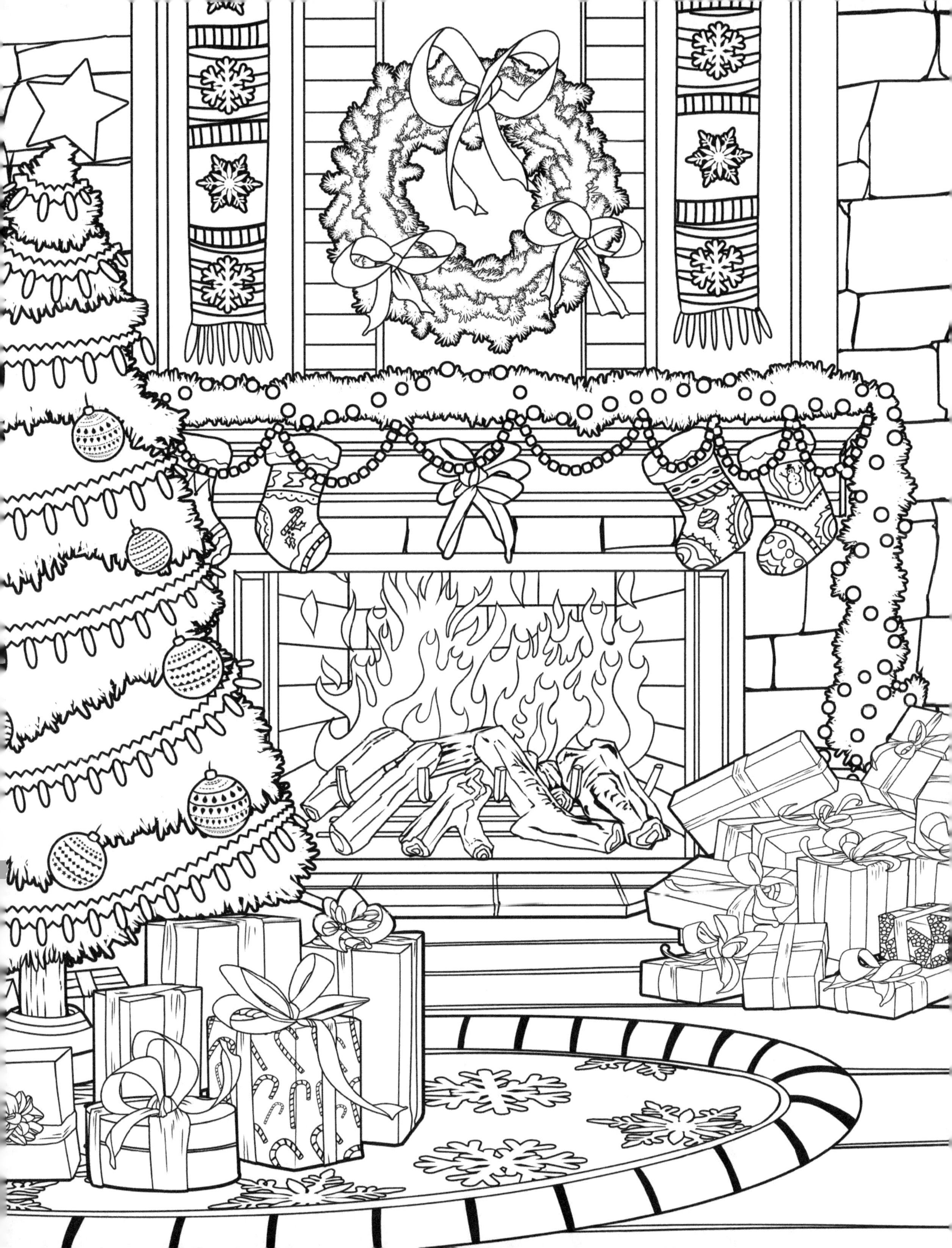

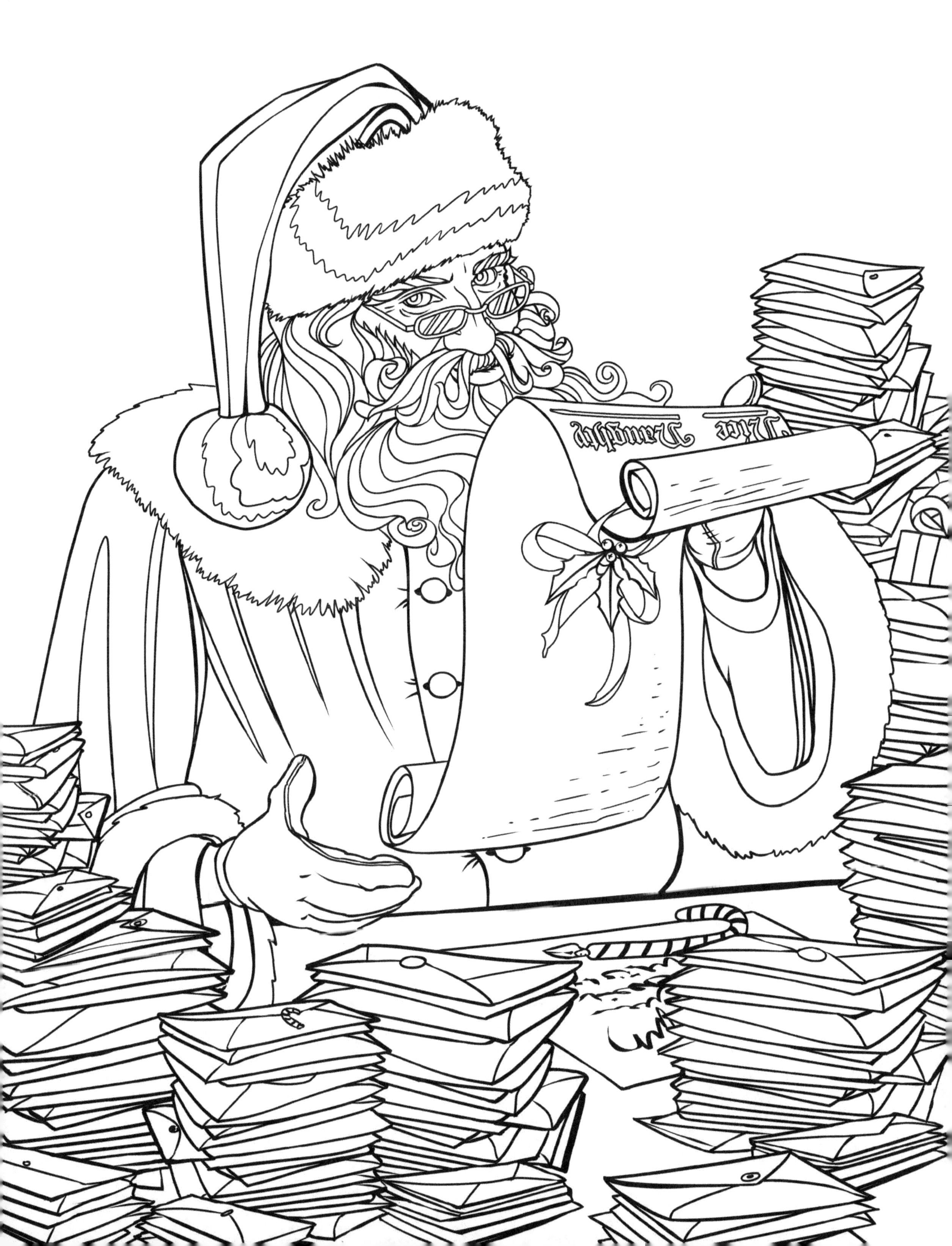
Nice Naughty

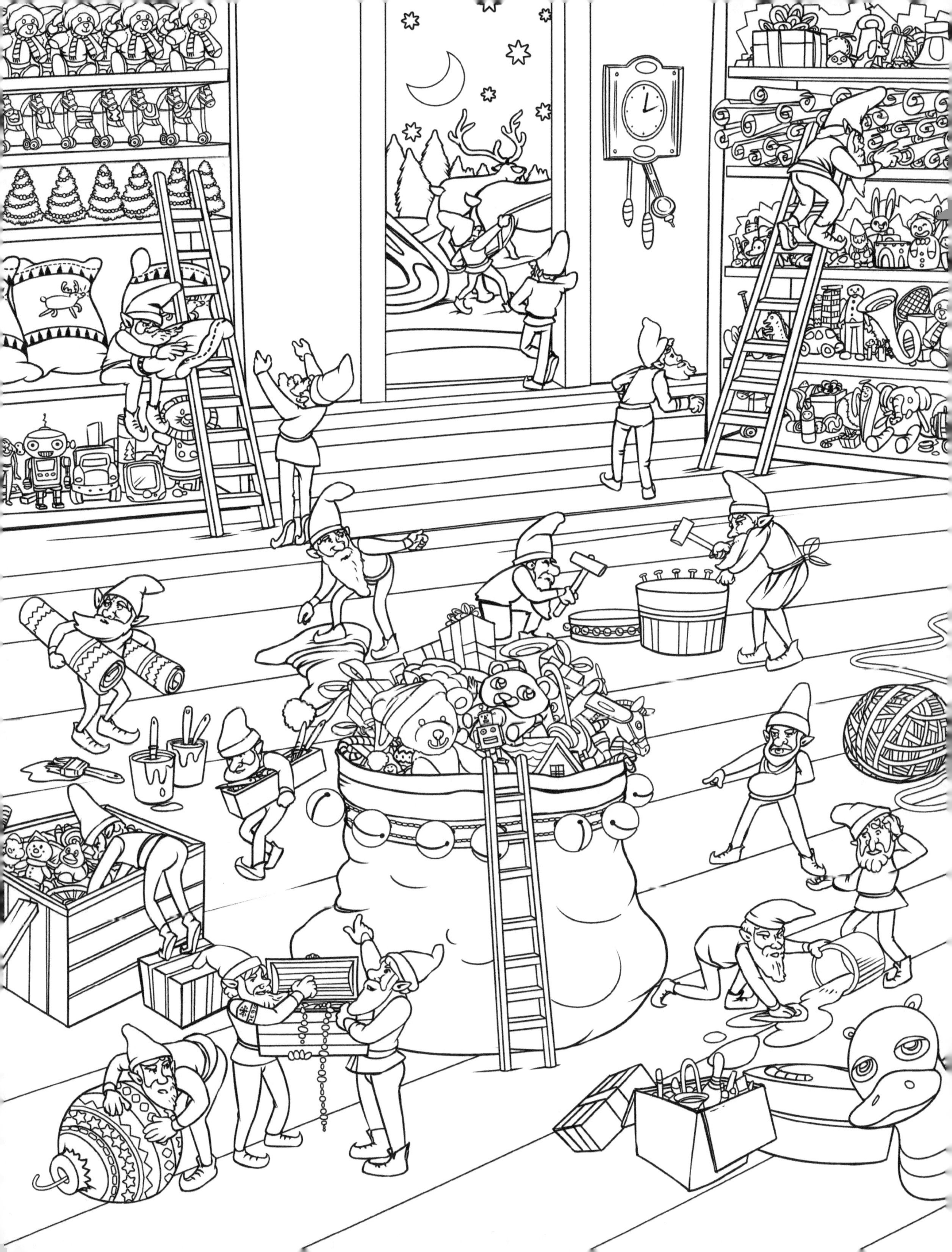

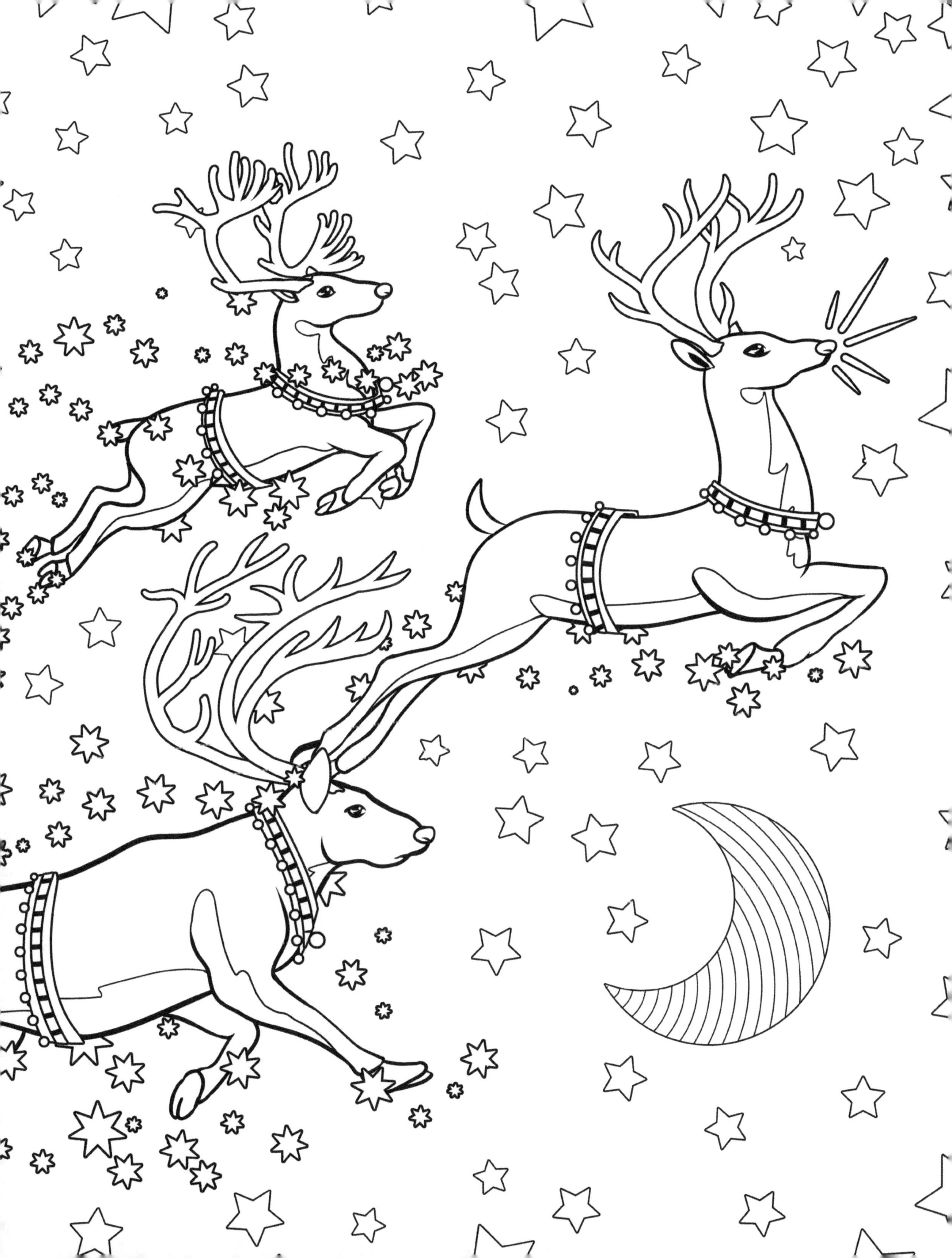

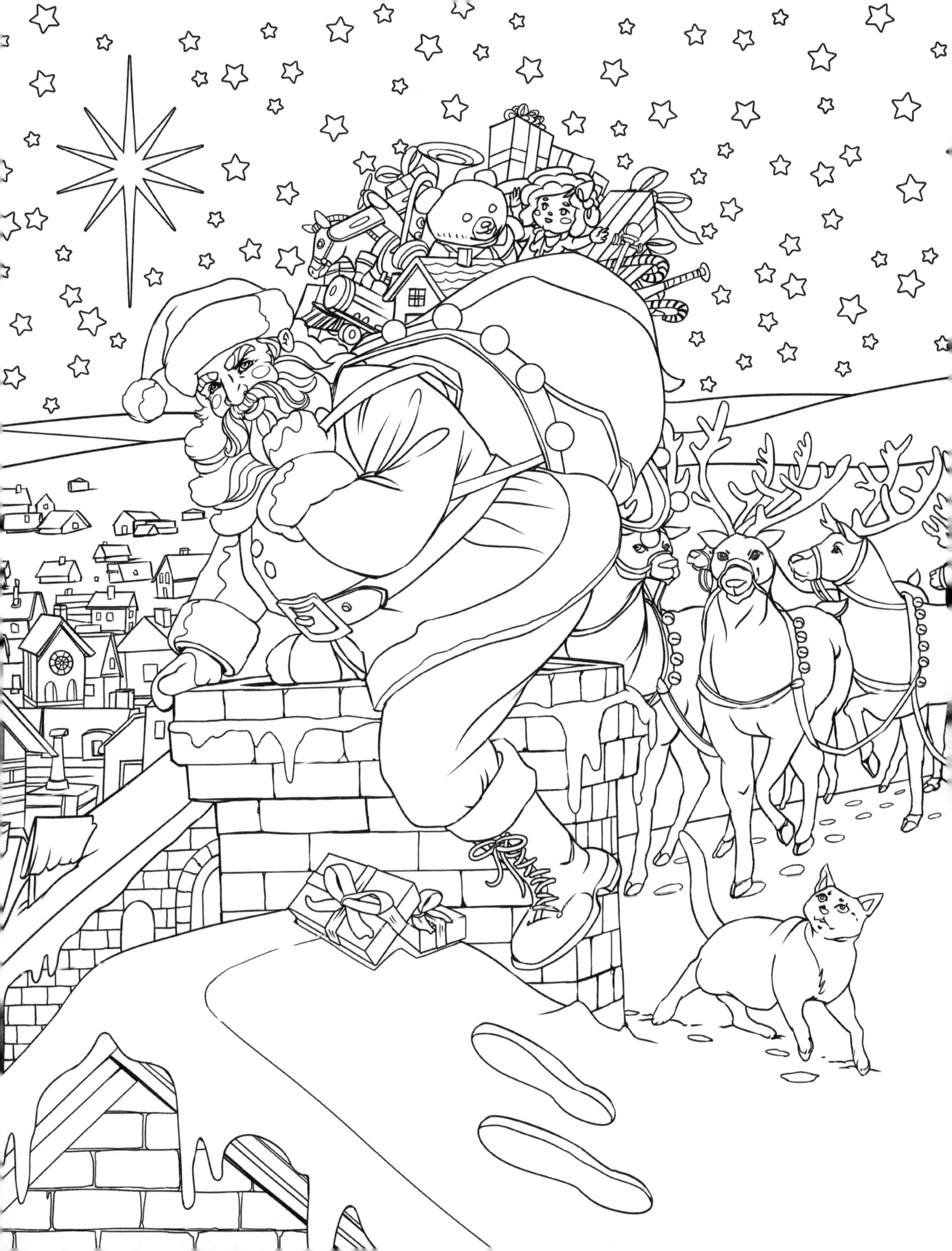

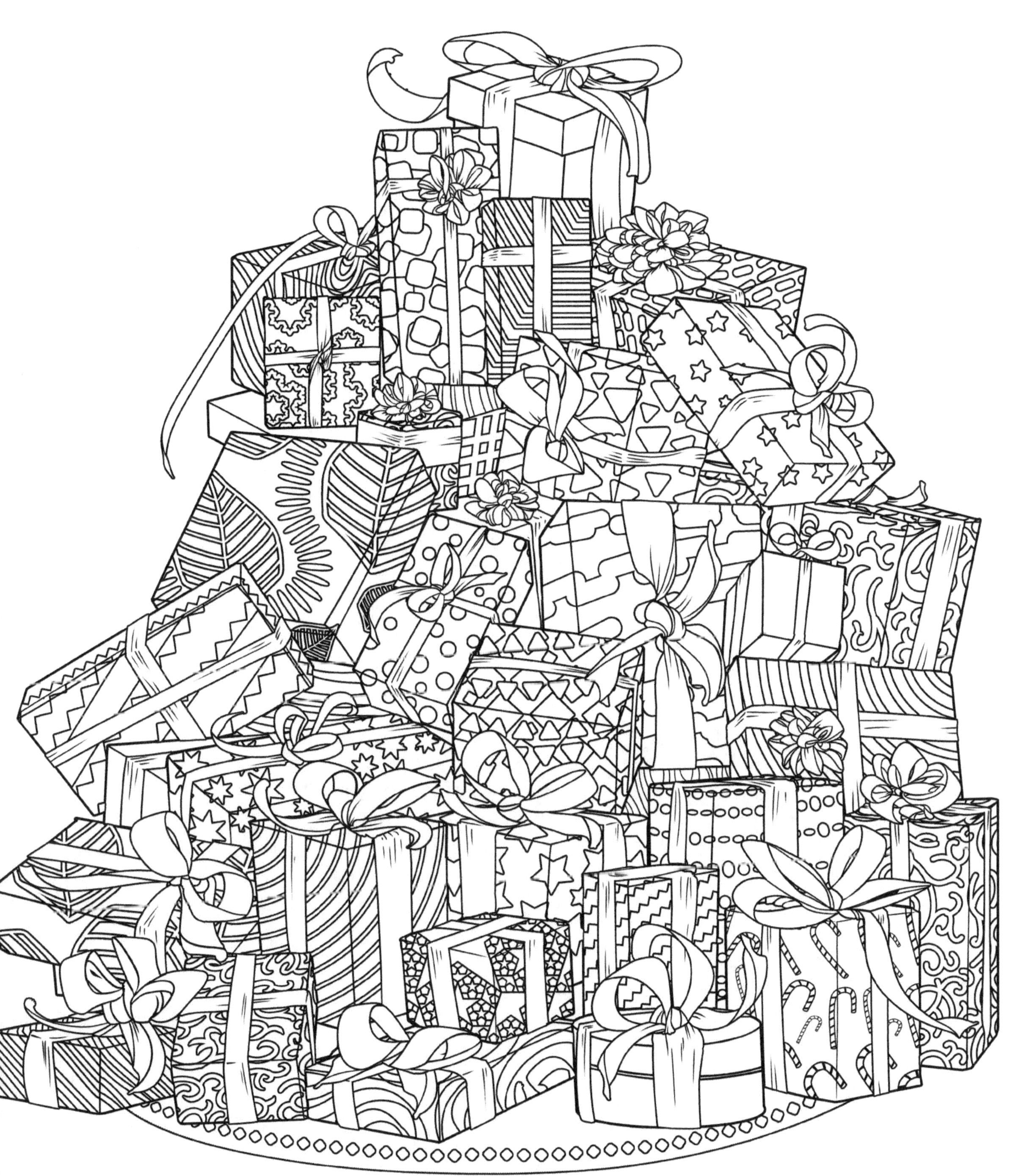

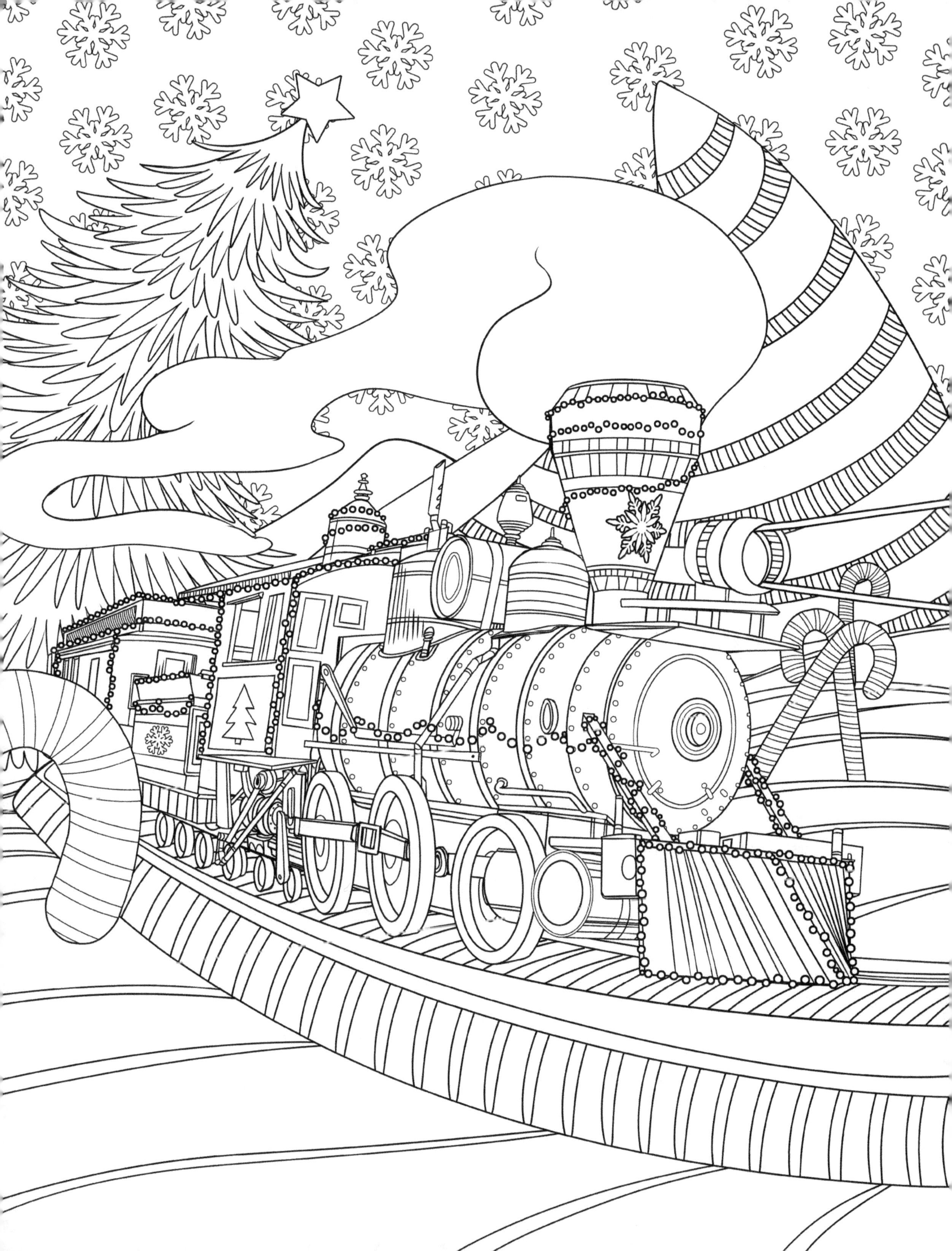

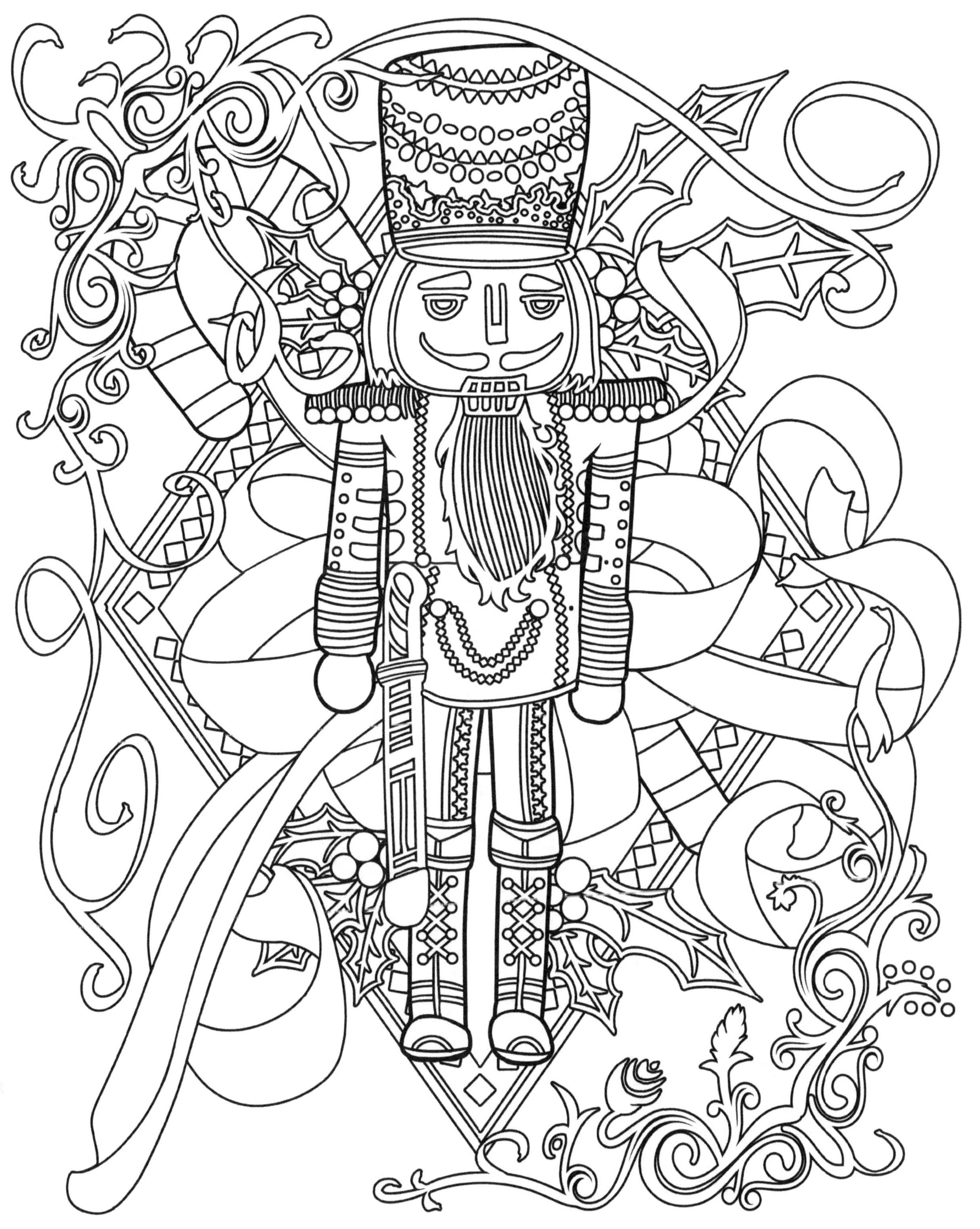

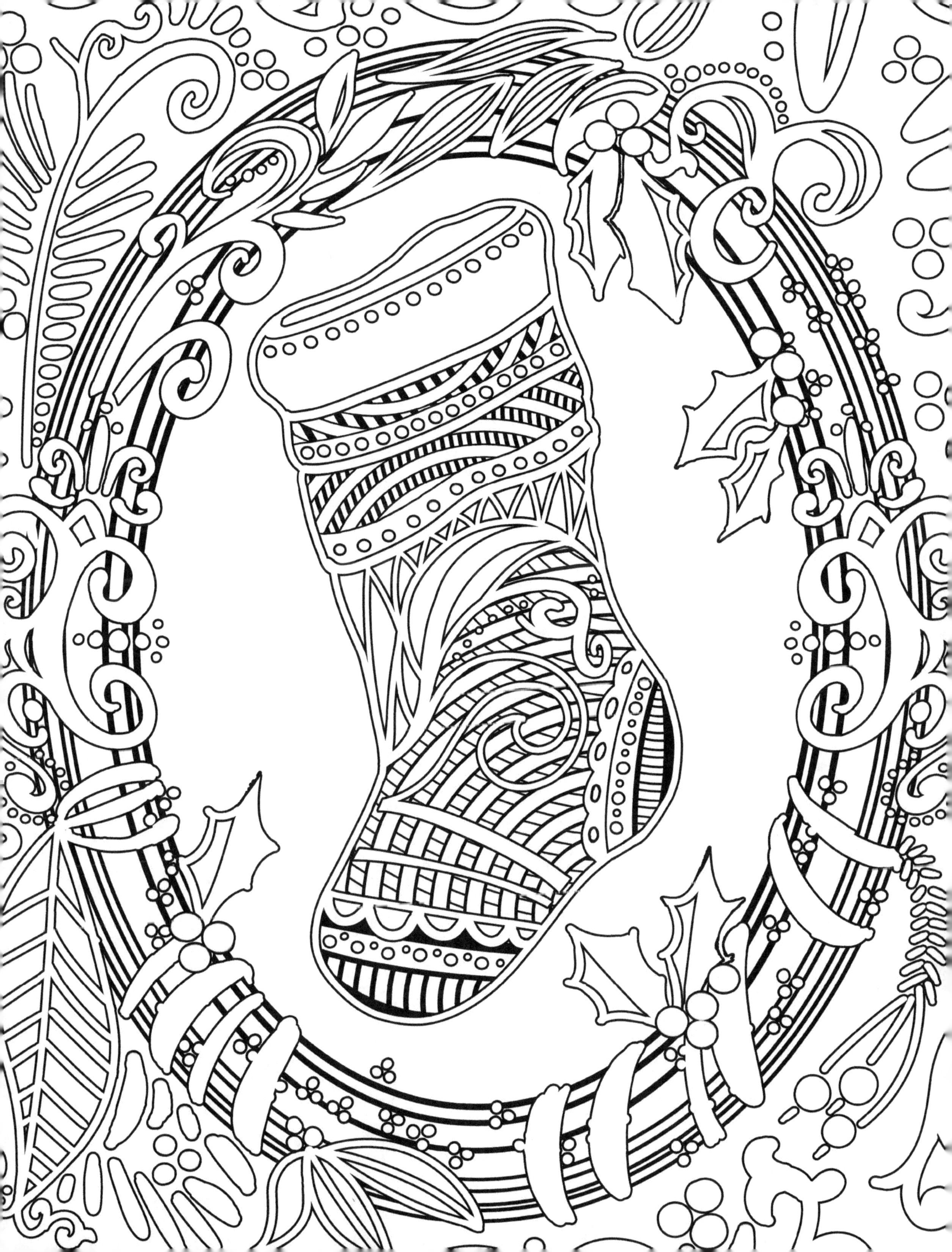

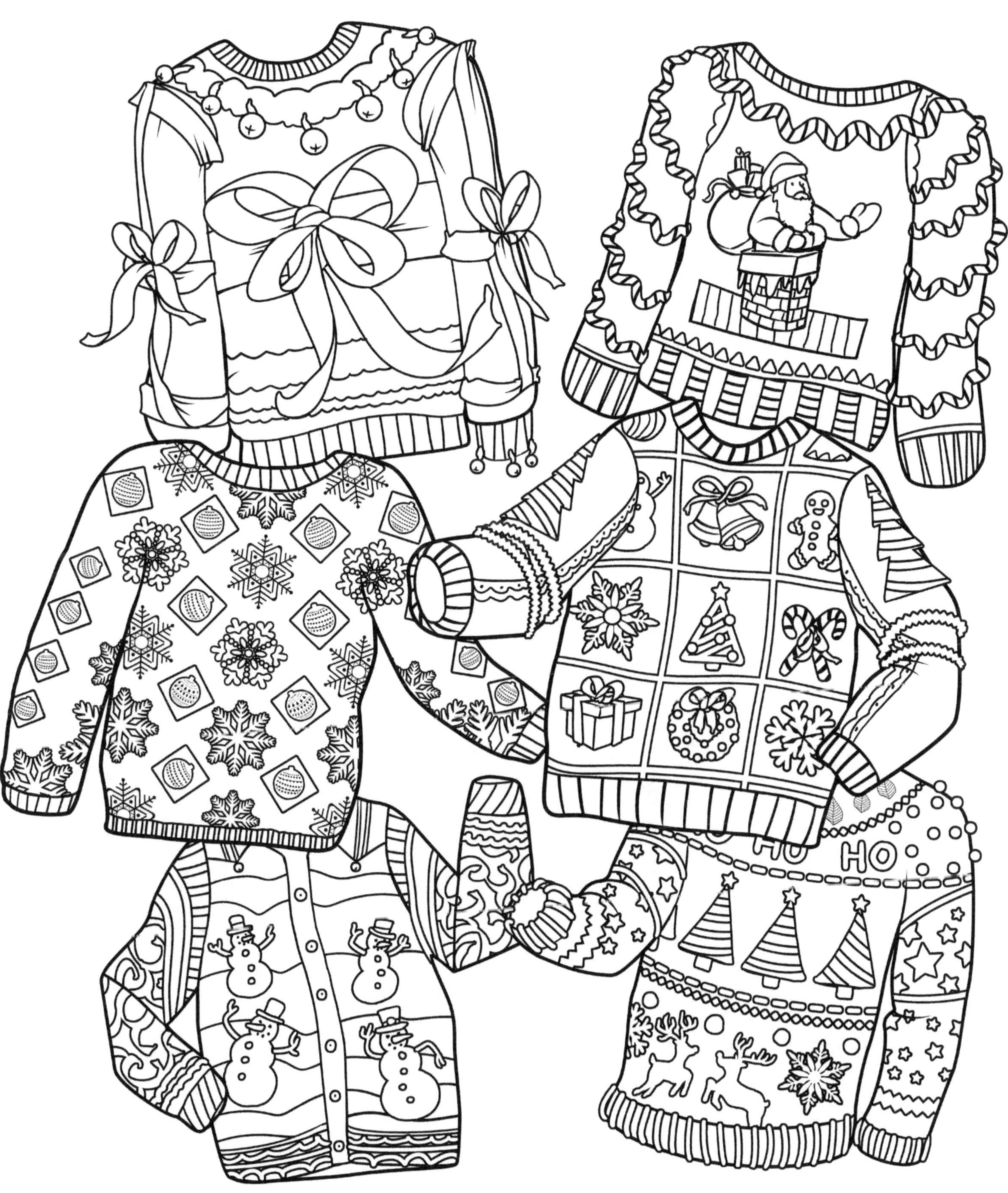
HO HO

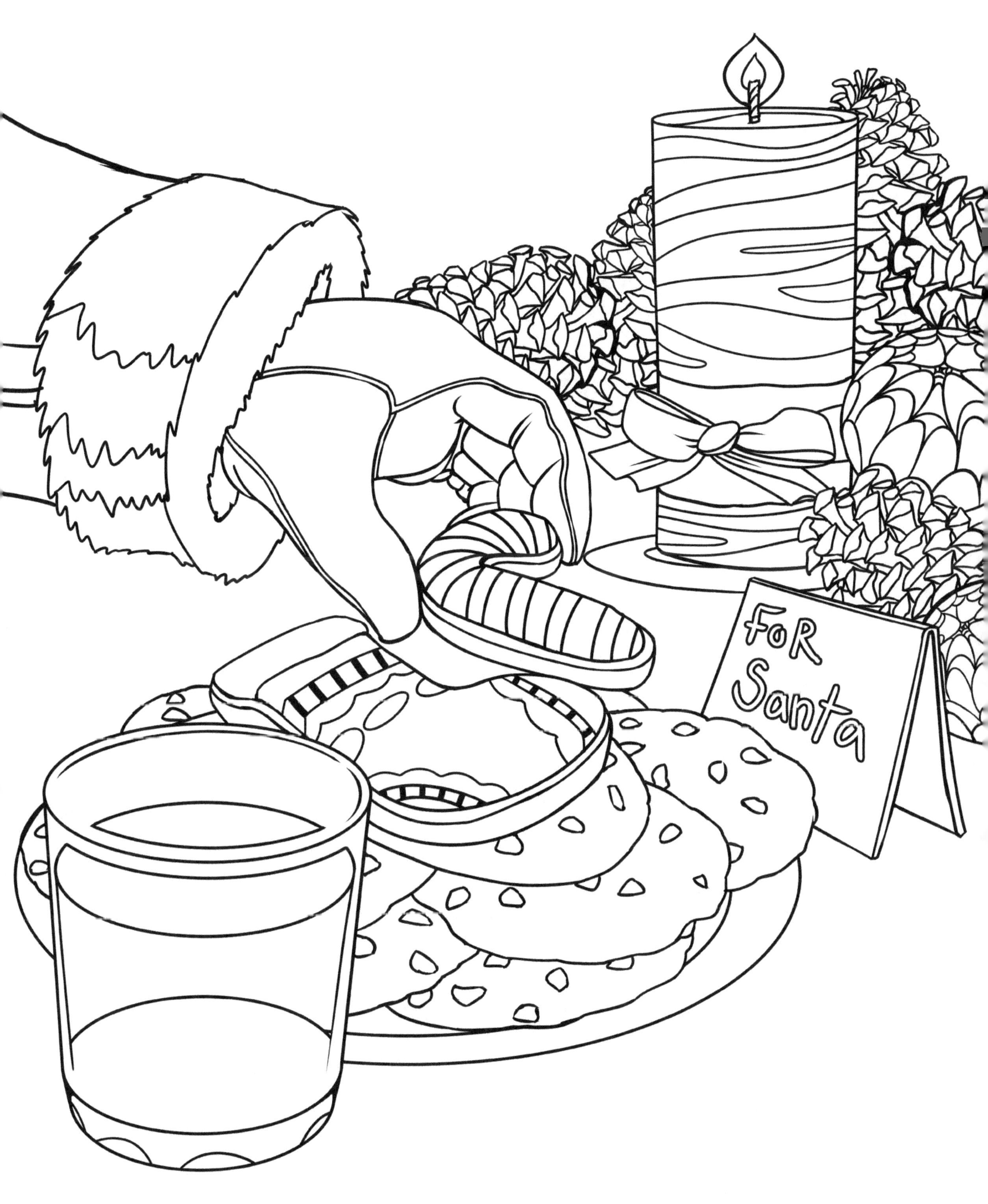
FoR
Santa

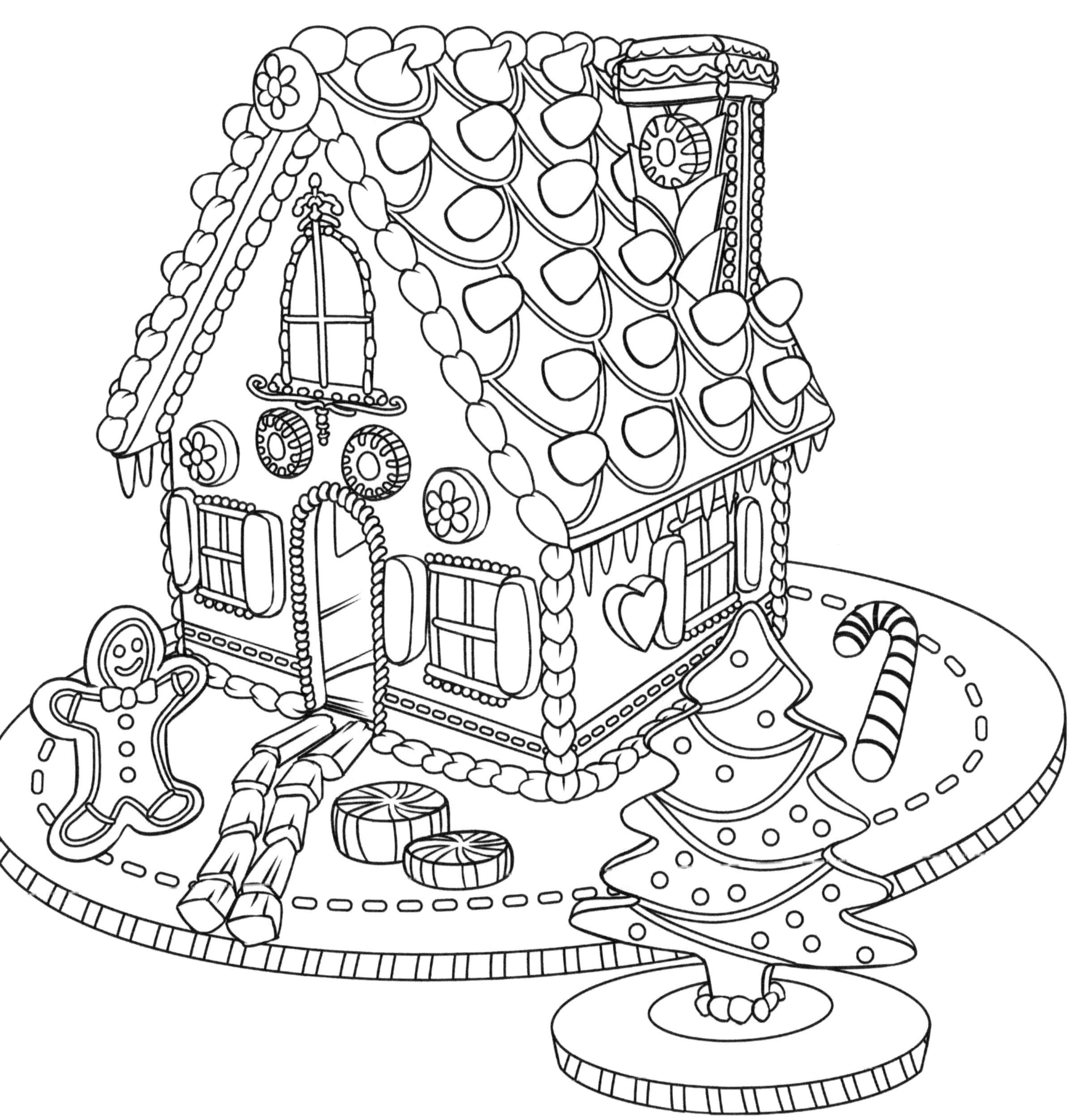

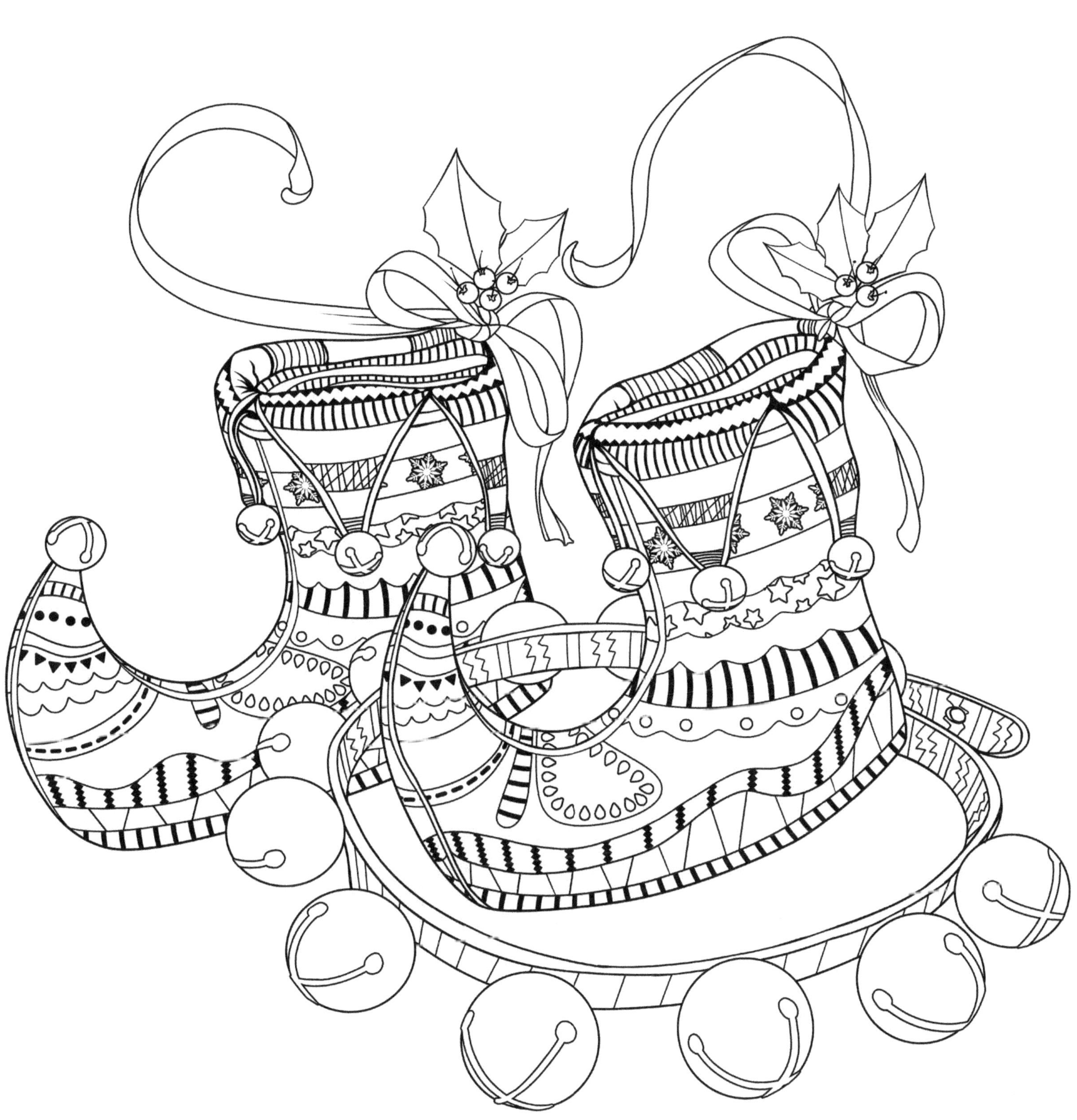

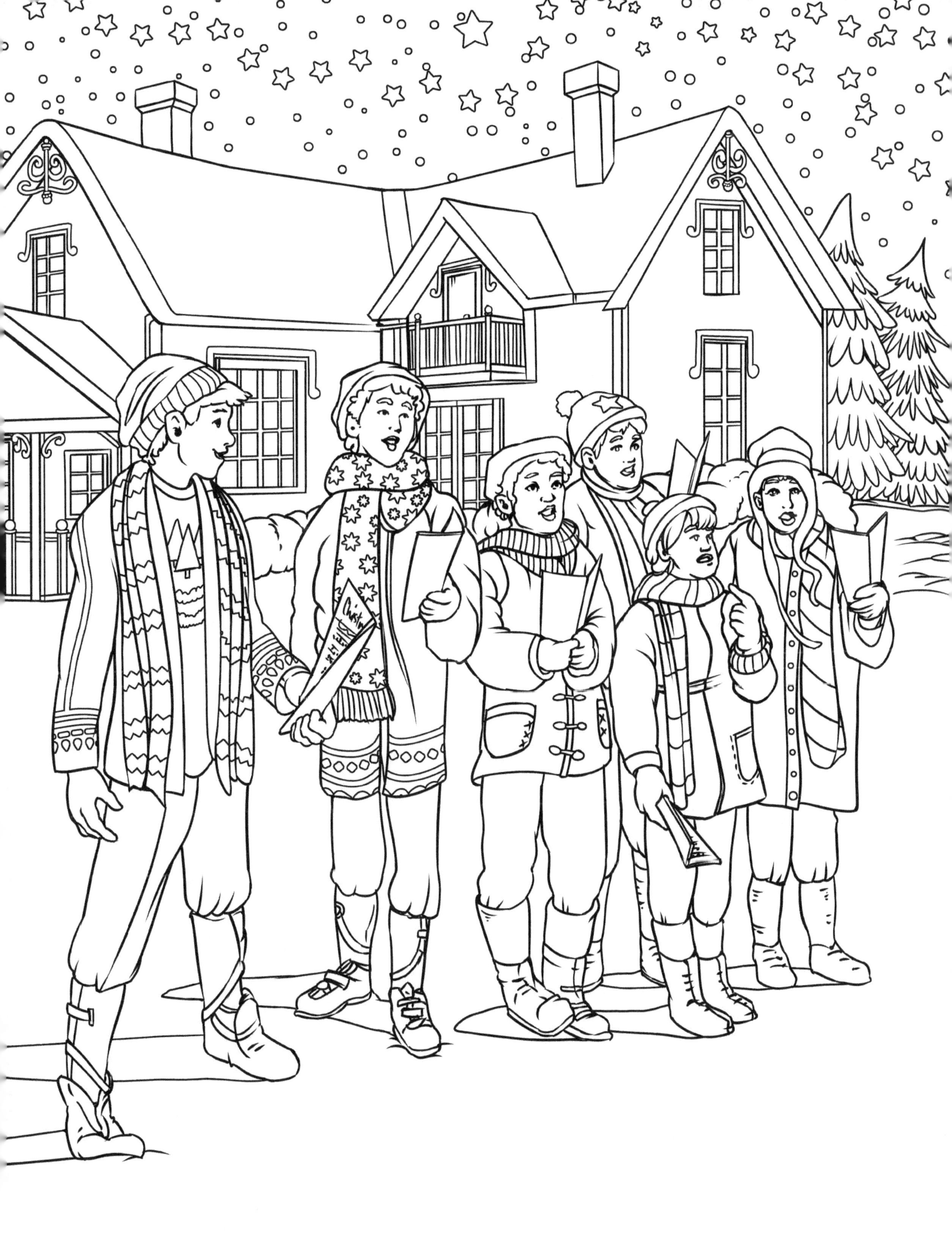

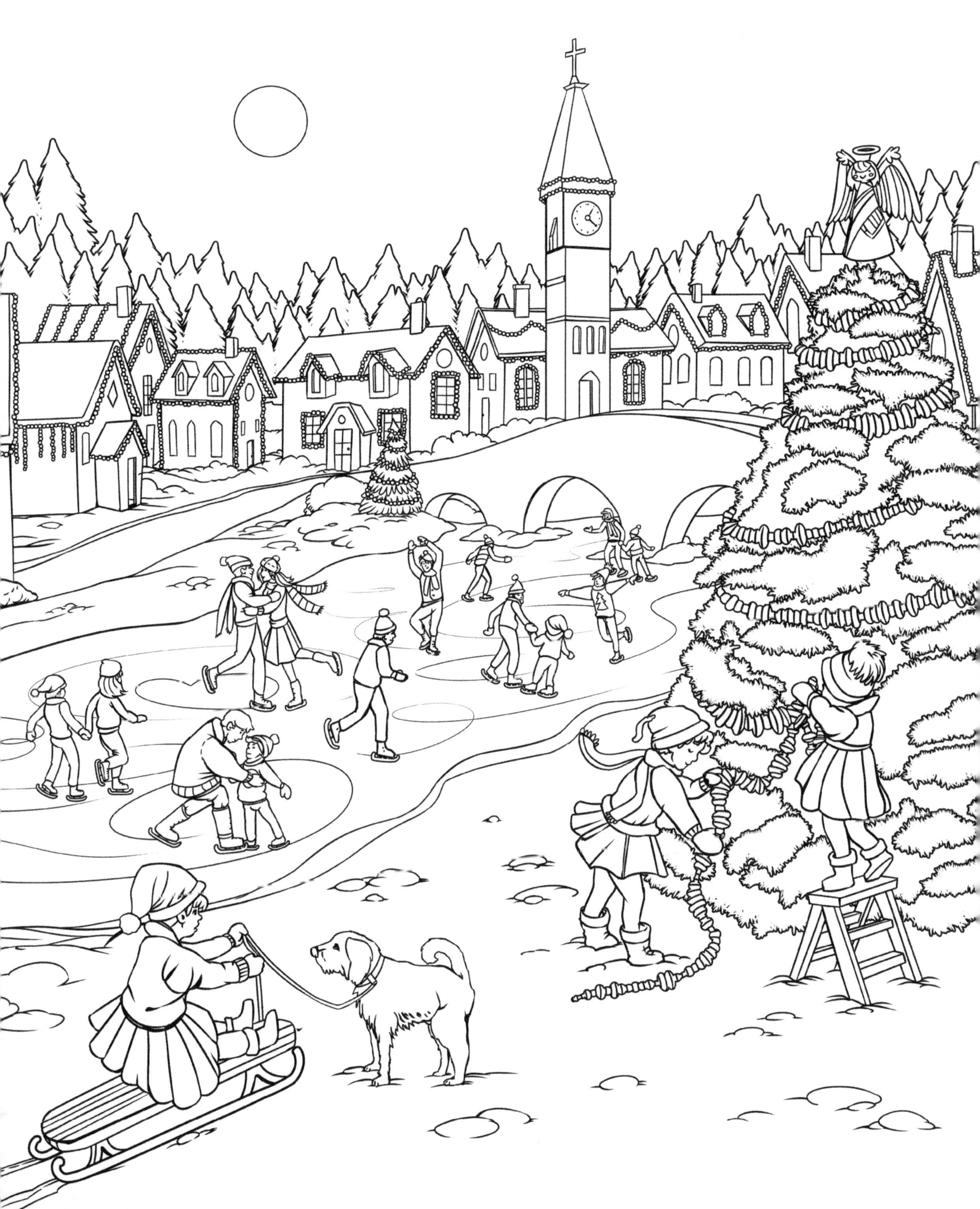

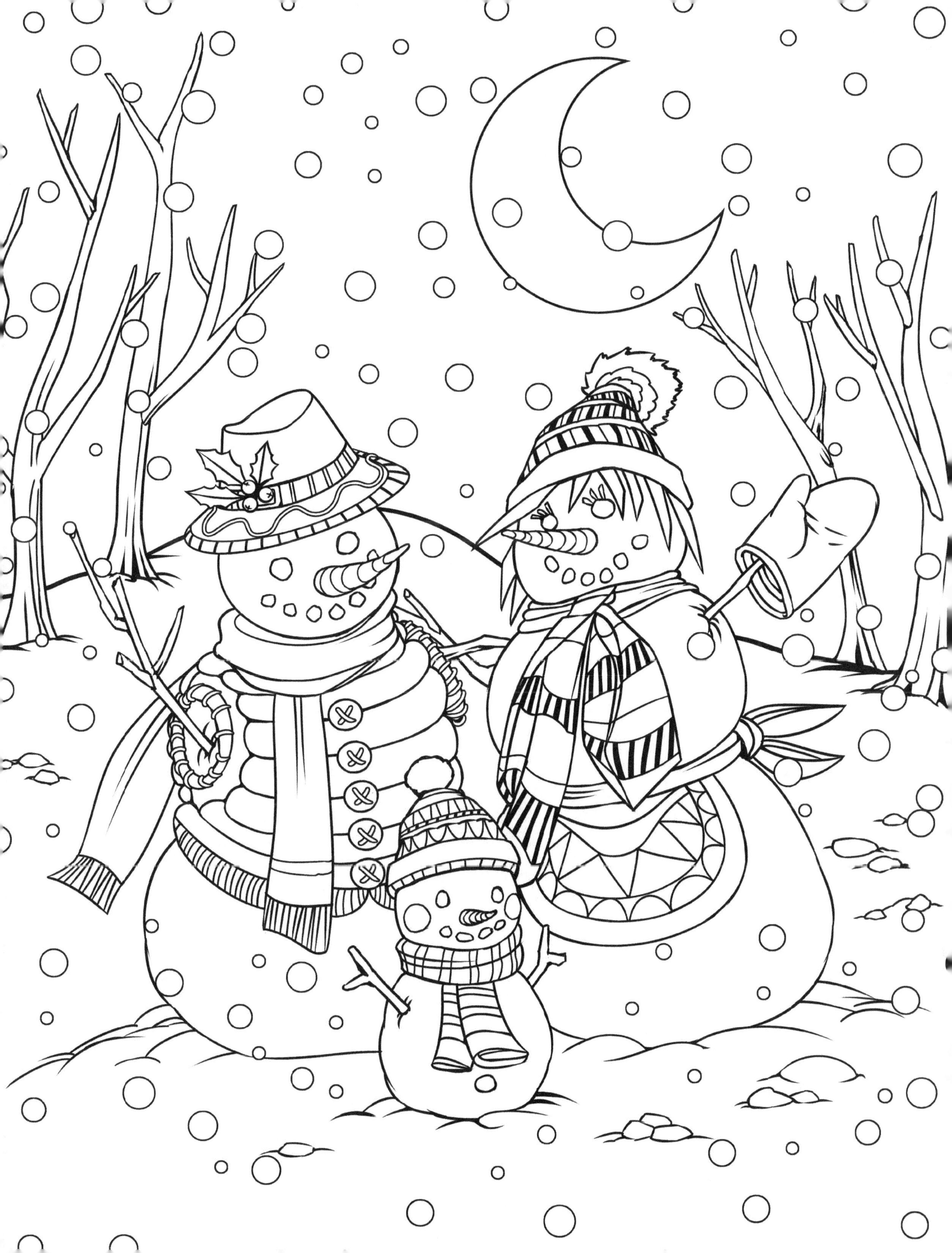

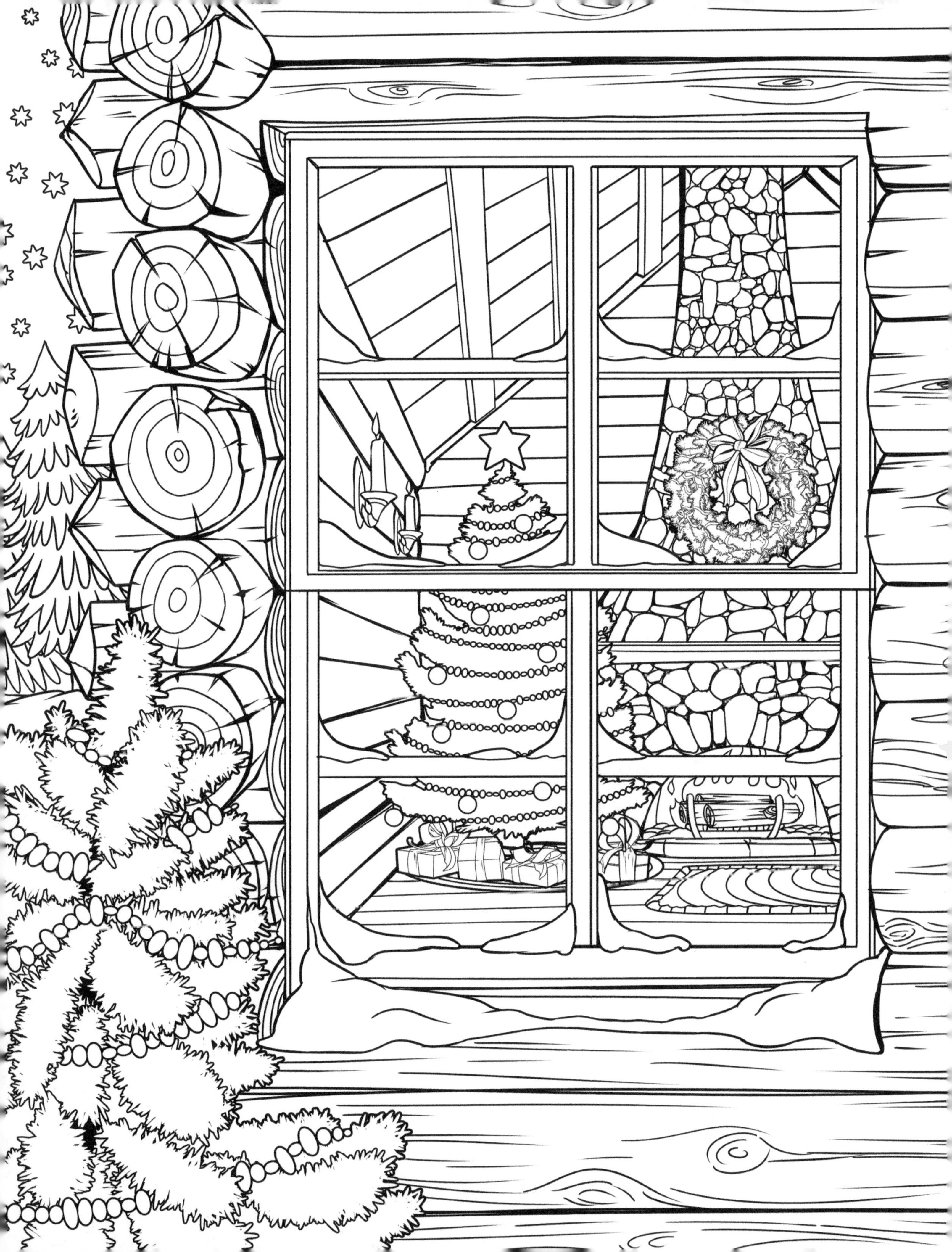

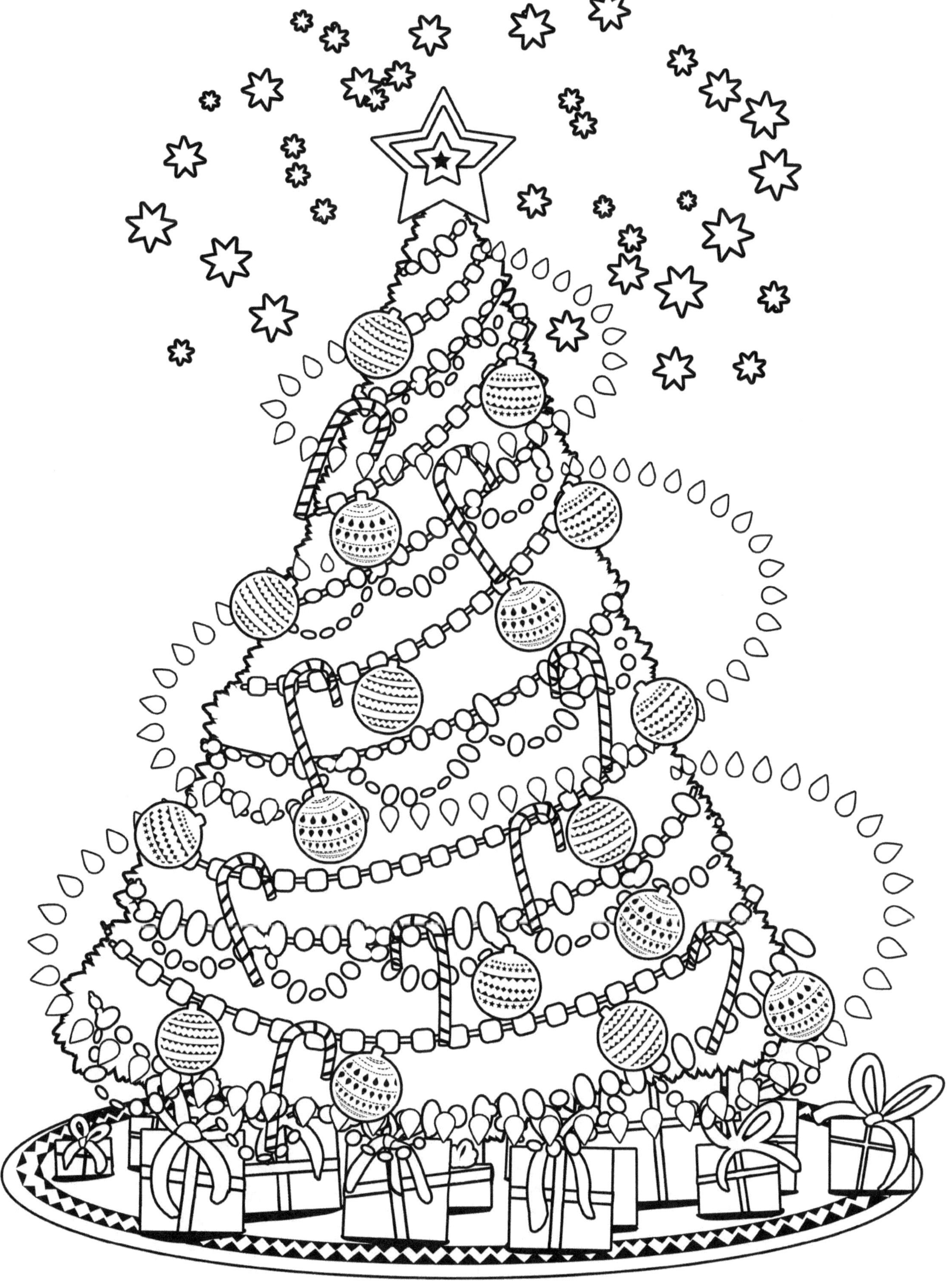

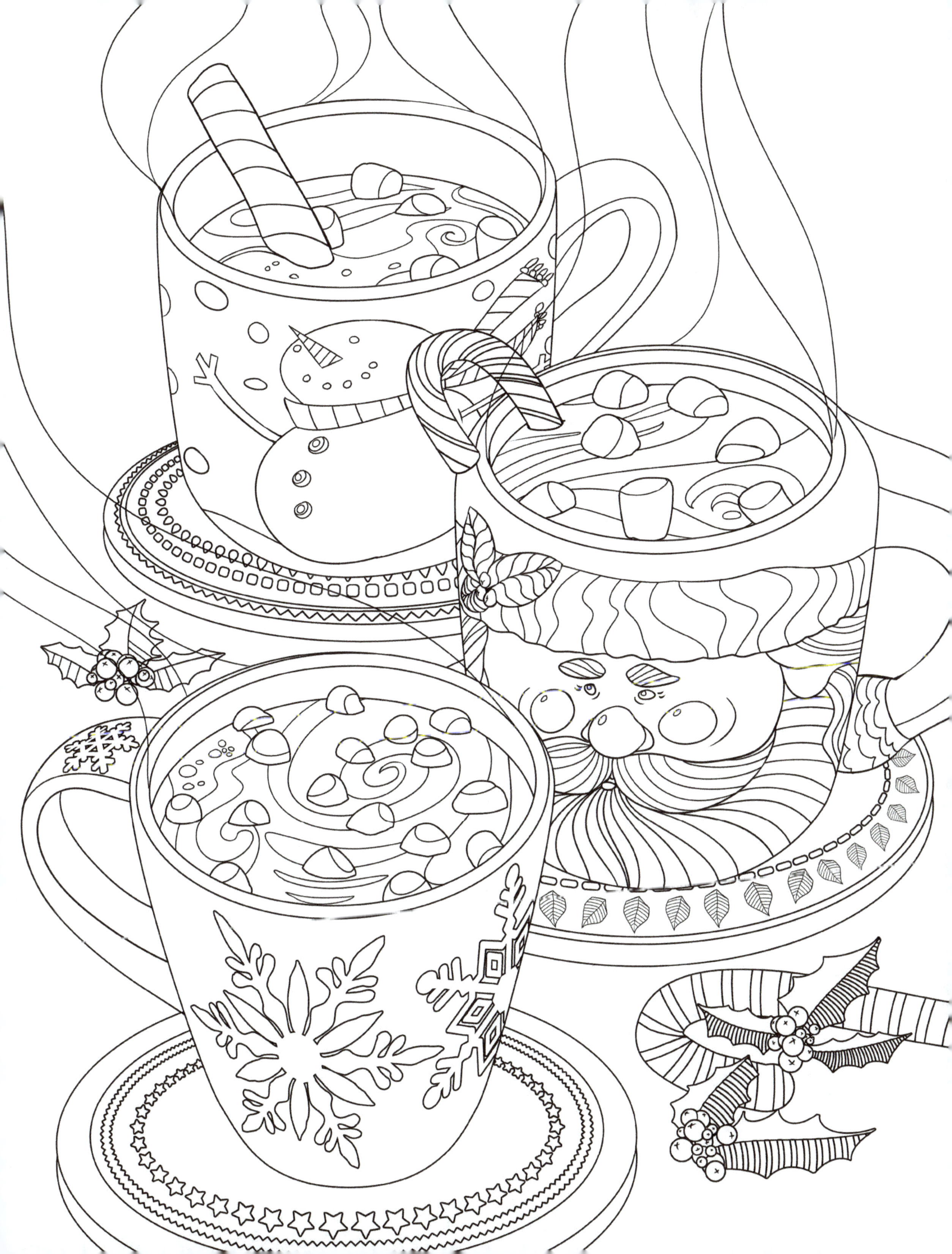

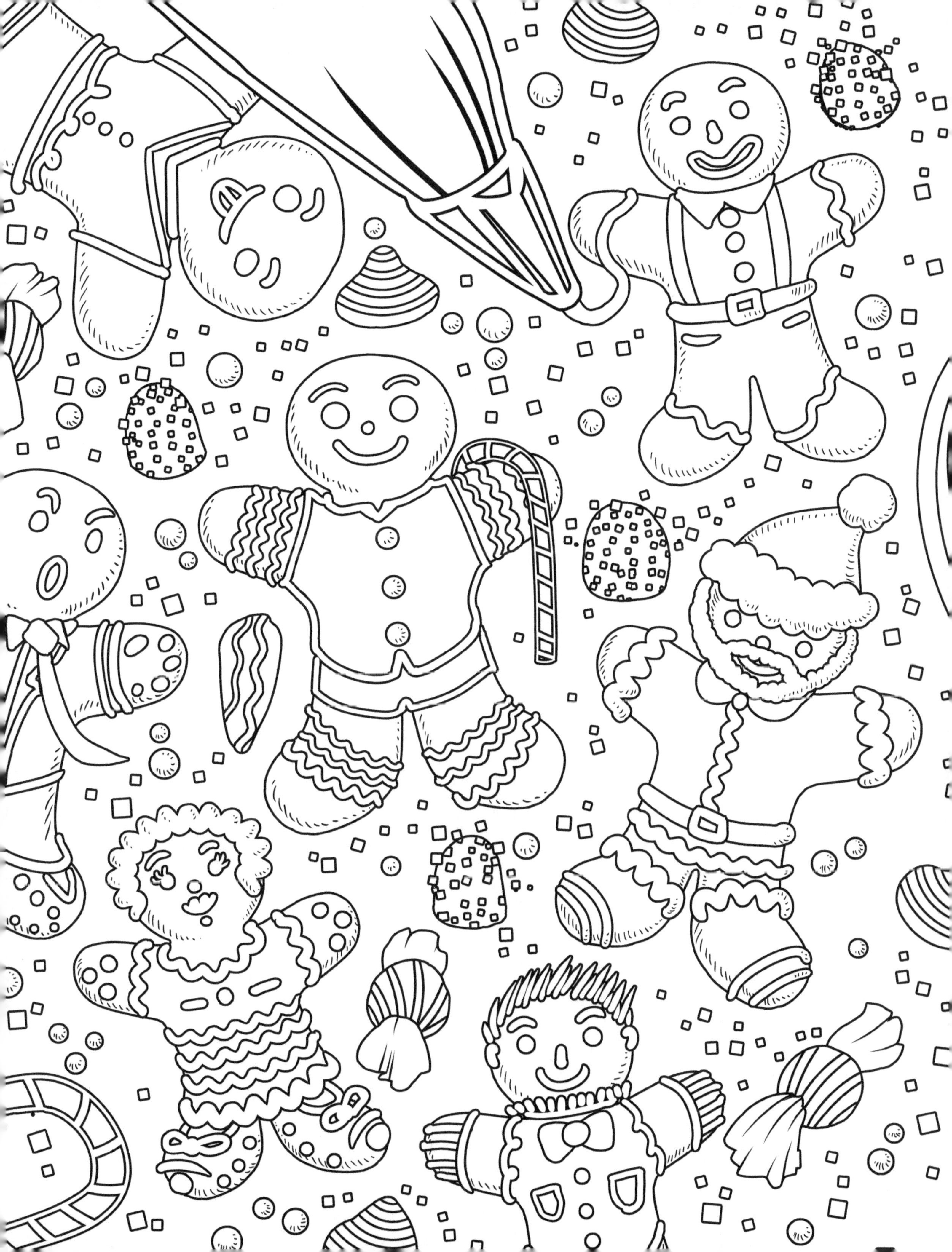

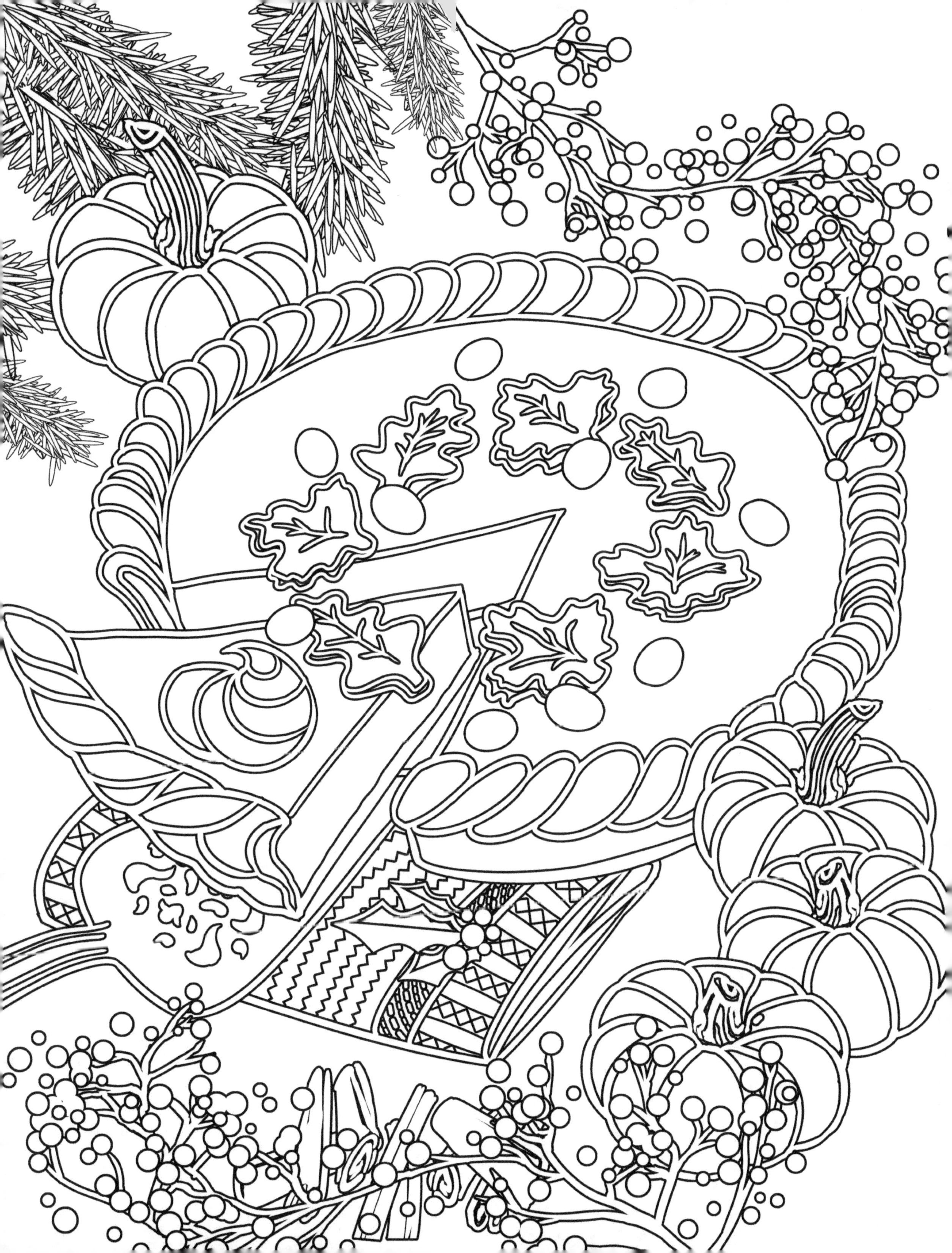

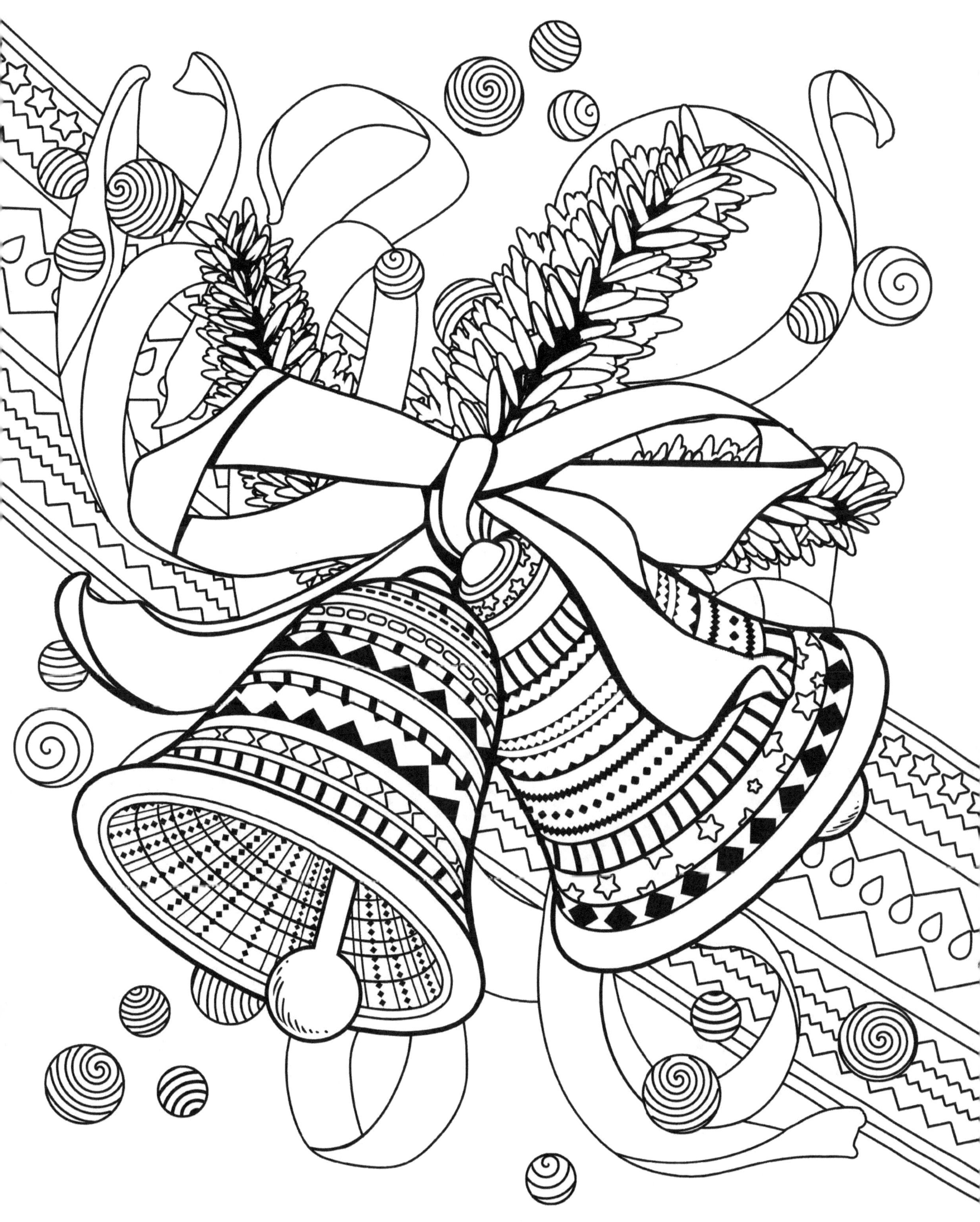

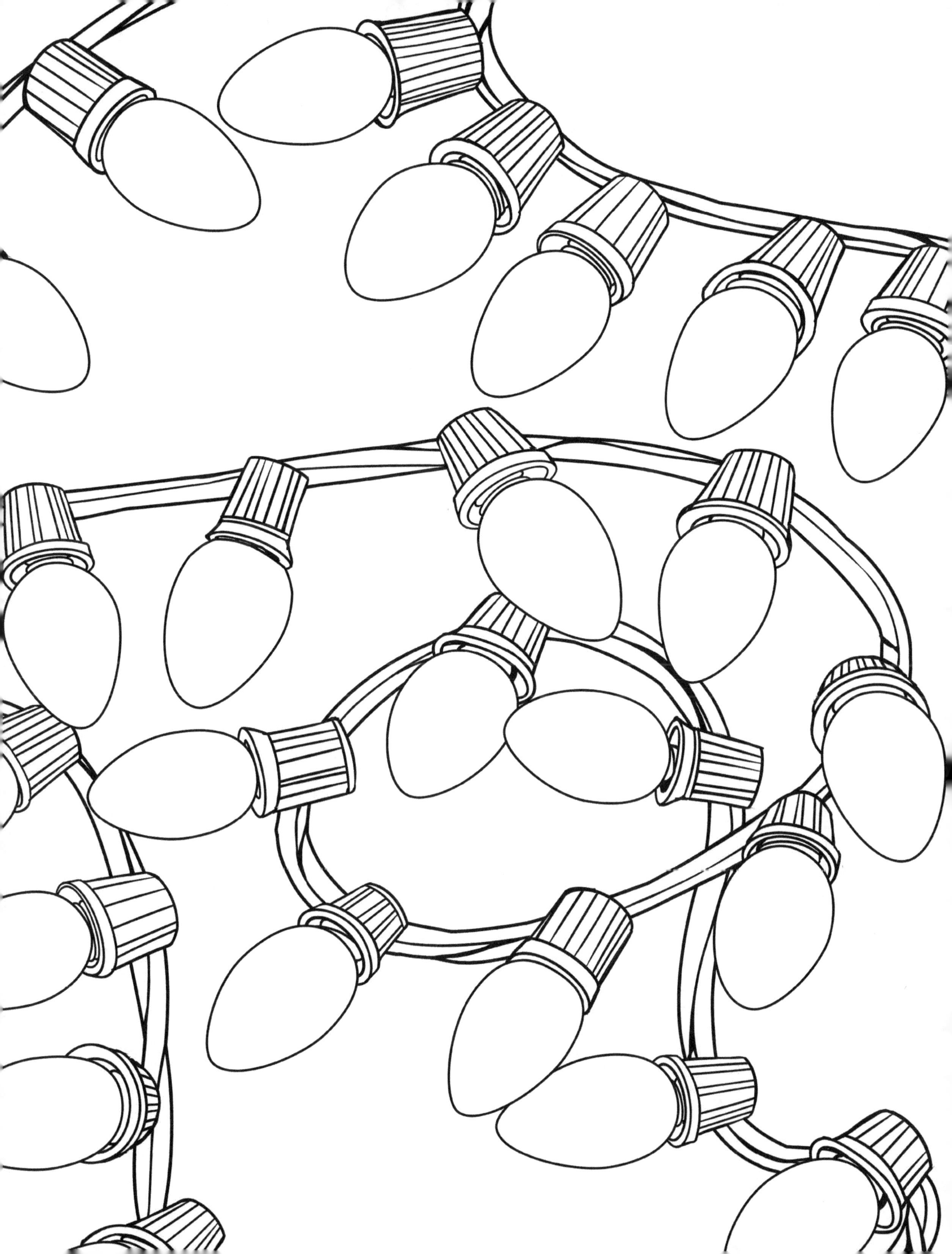

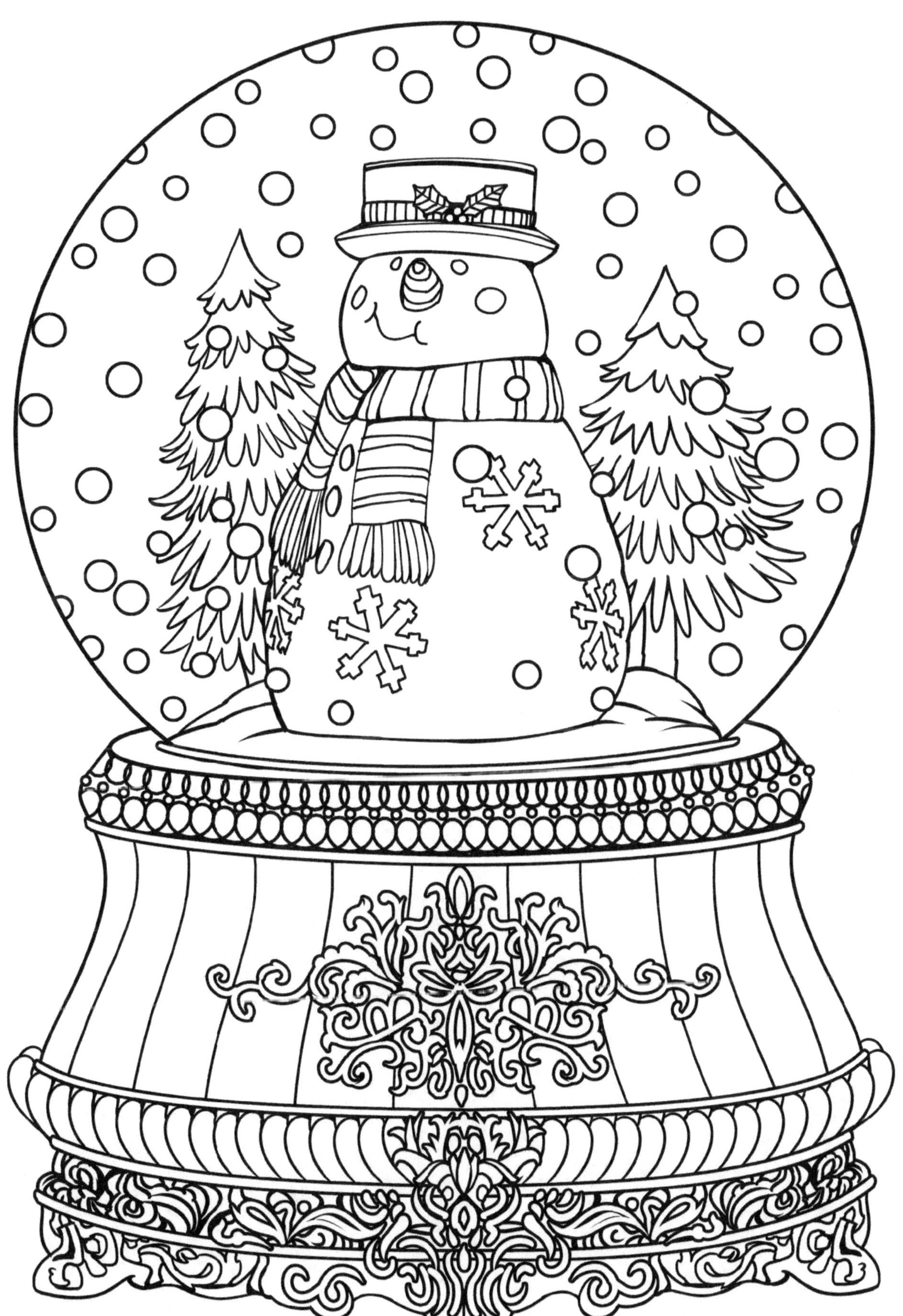

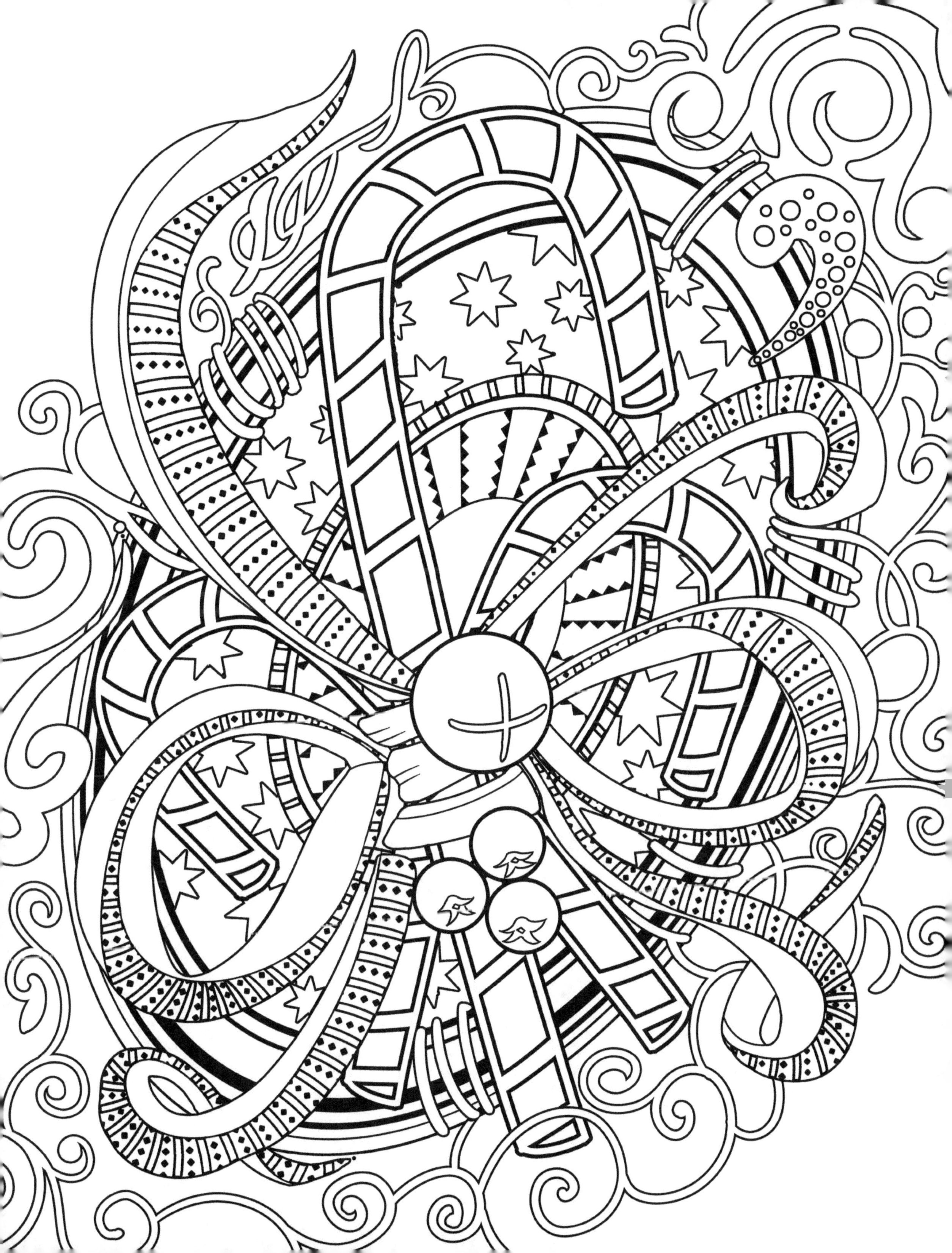

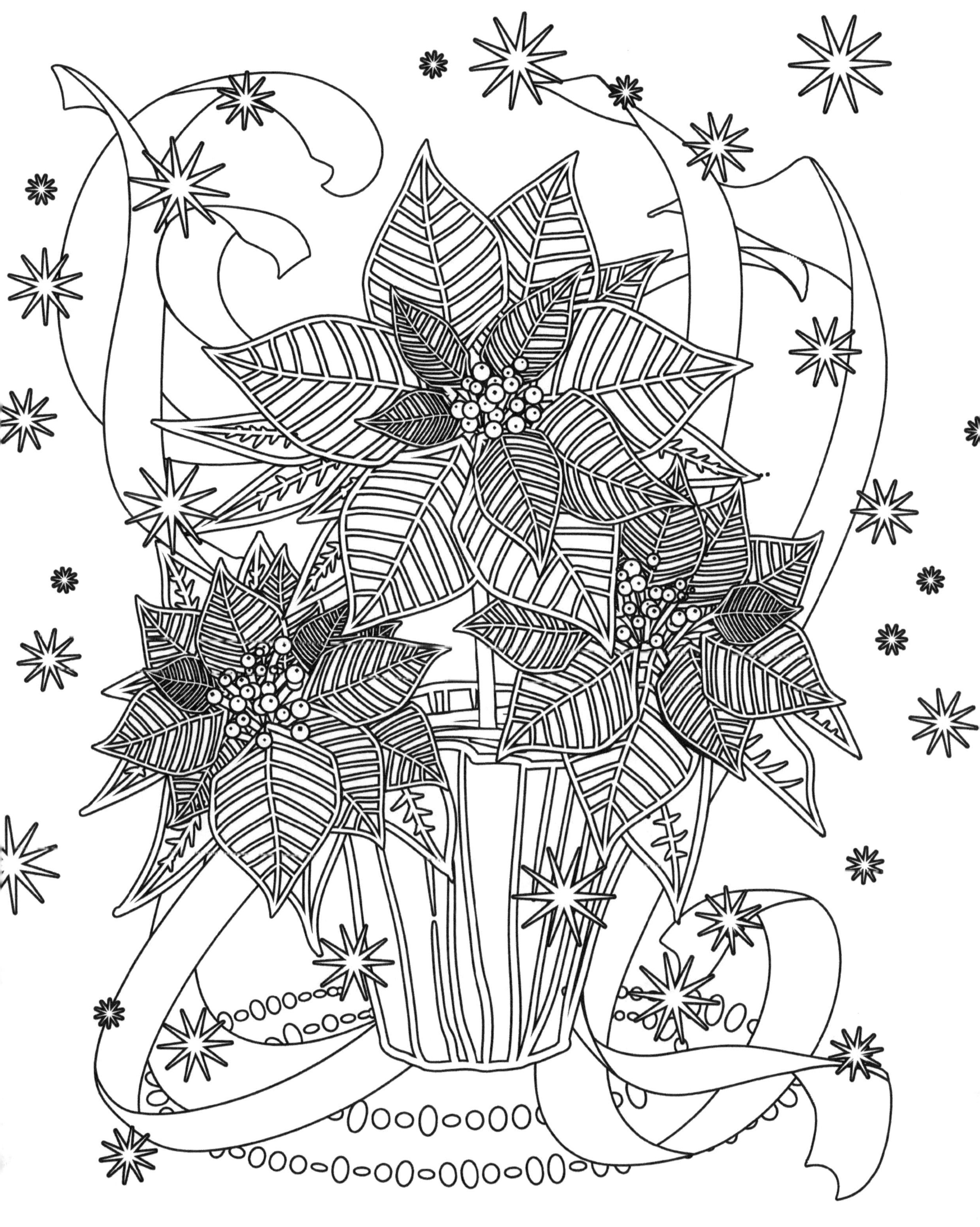

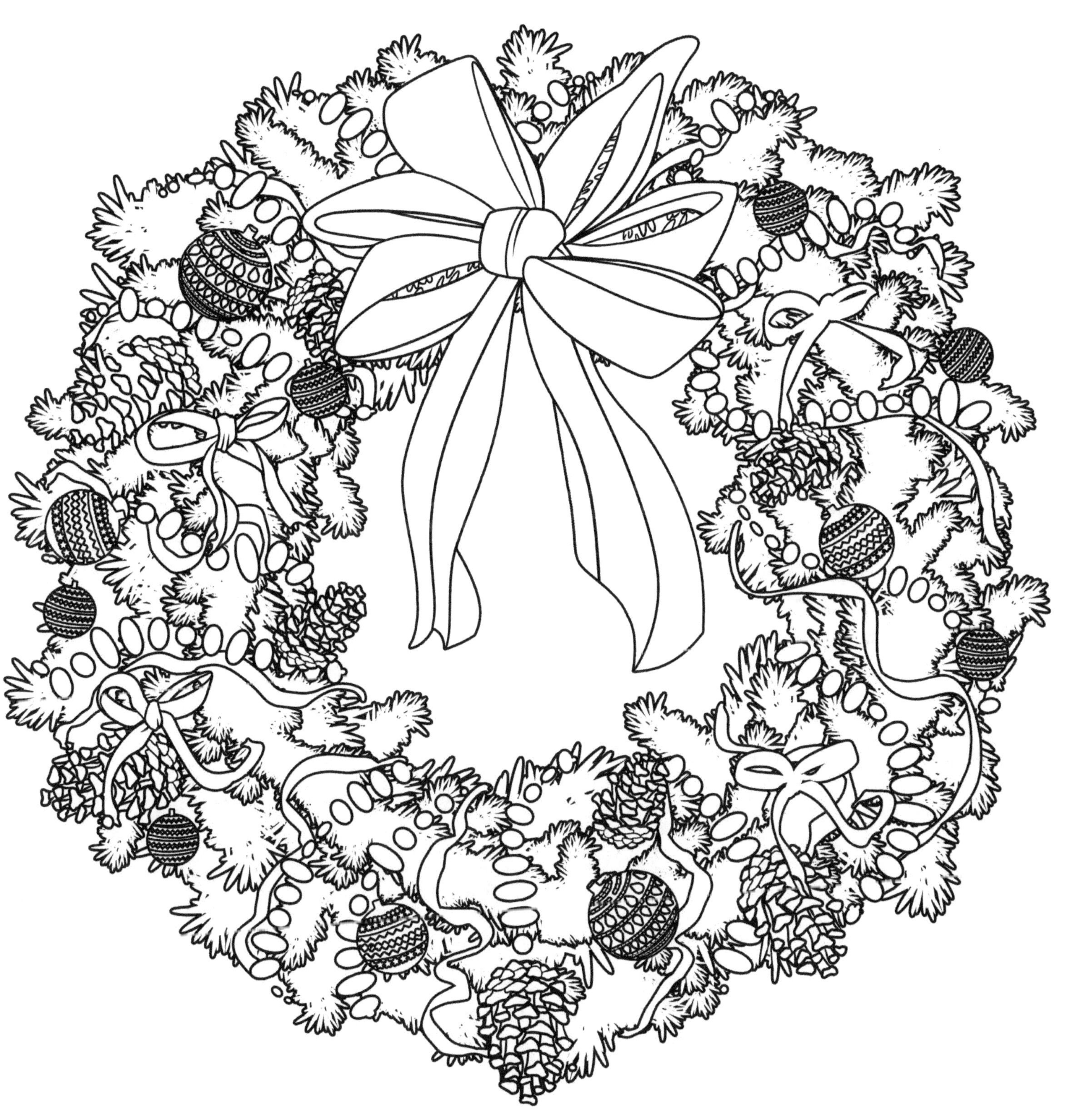

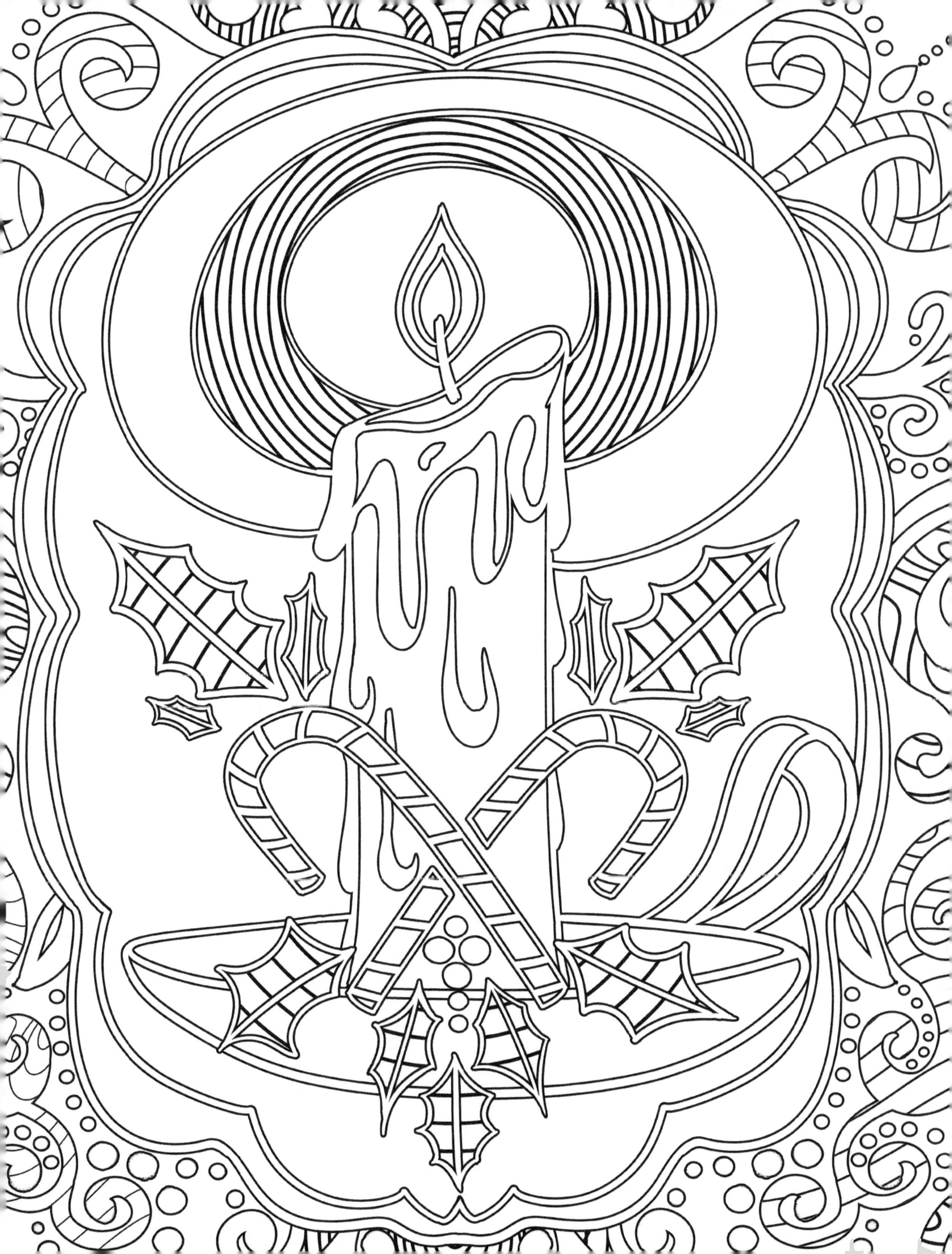

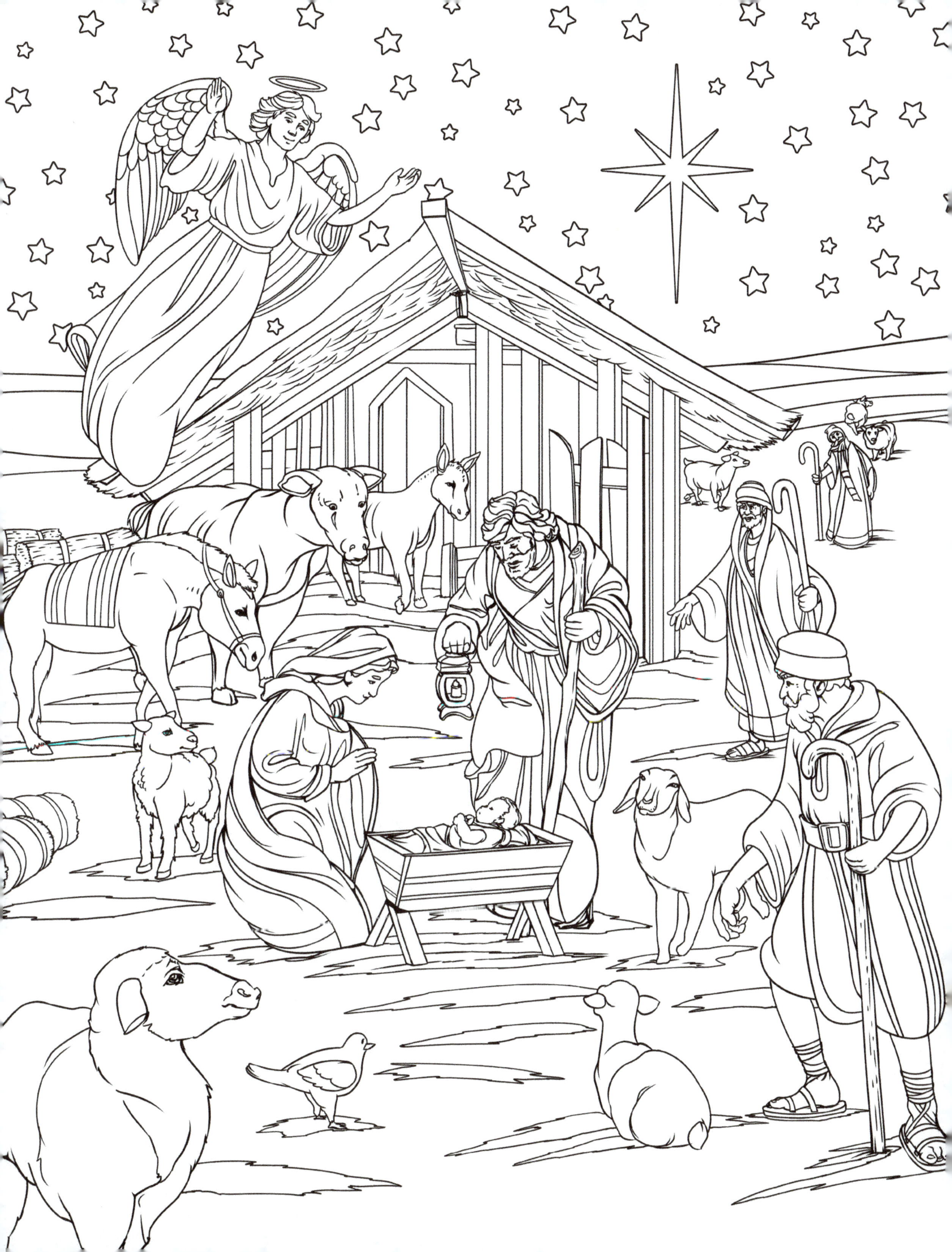

Bonus Christmas Kaleidoscopes

Relax and reflect as you color in the following
10 free bonus Christmas Kaleidoscope illustrations!

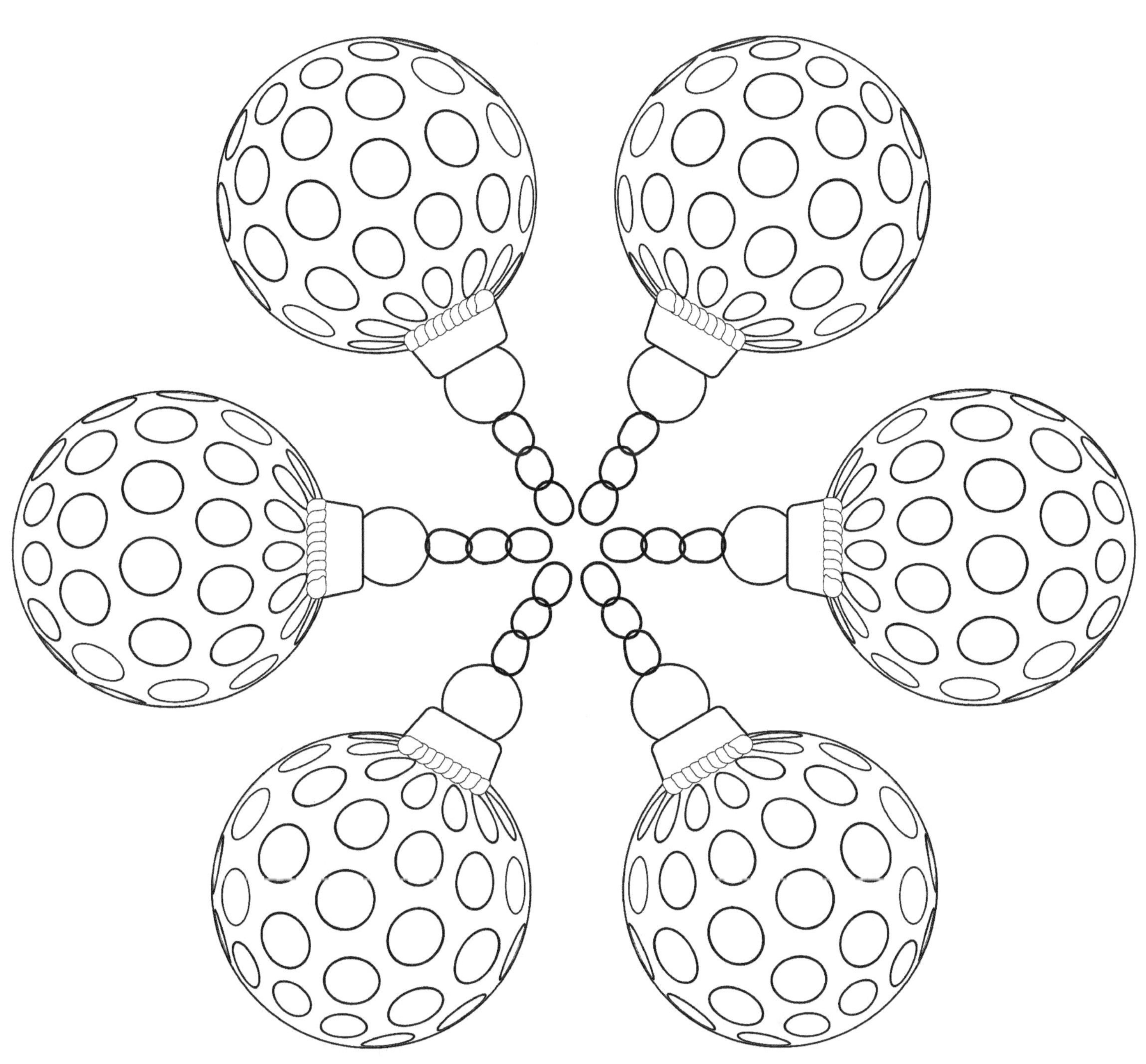

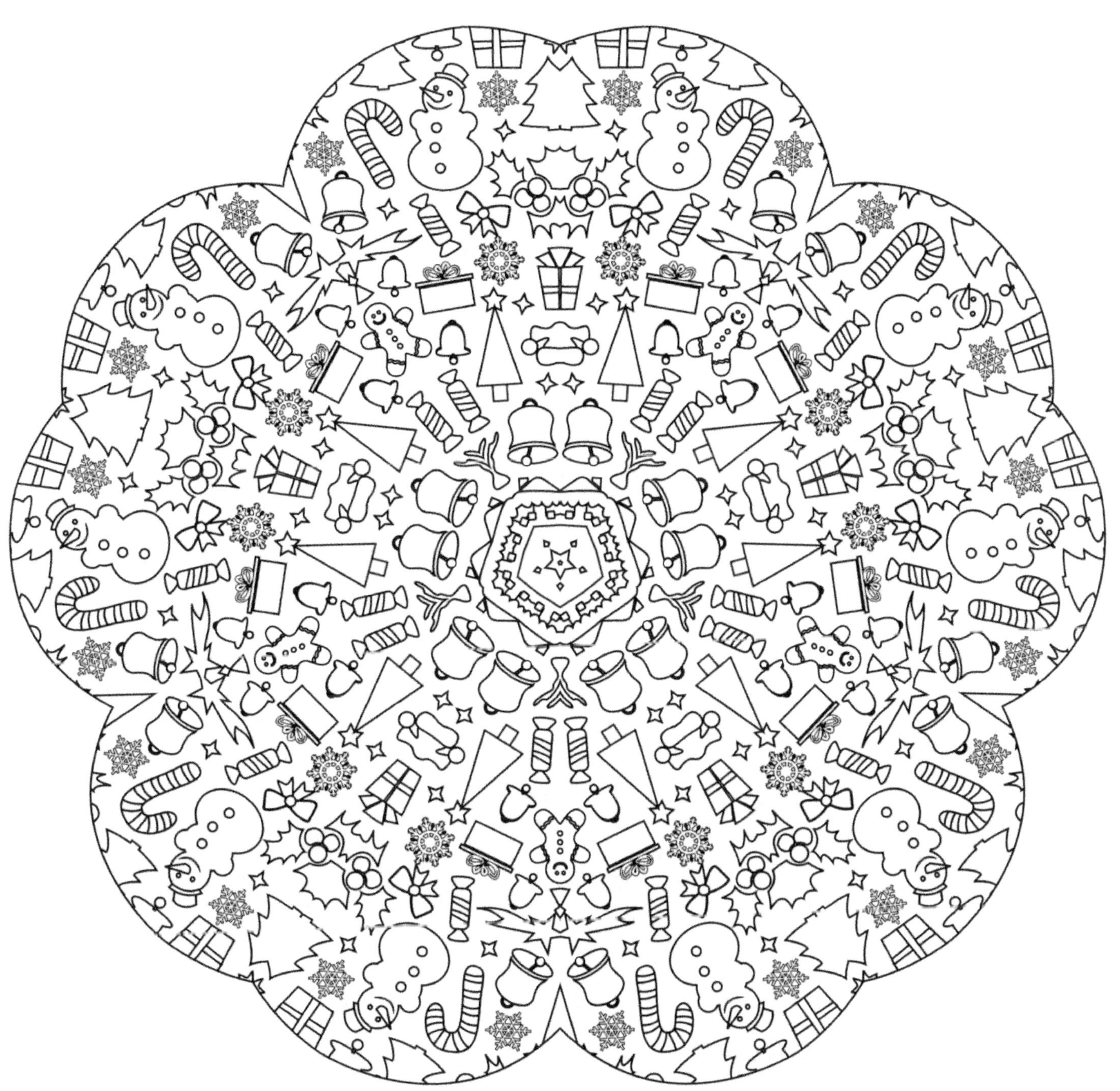

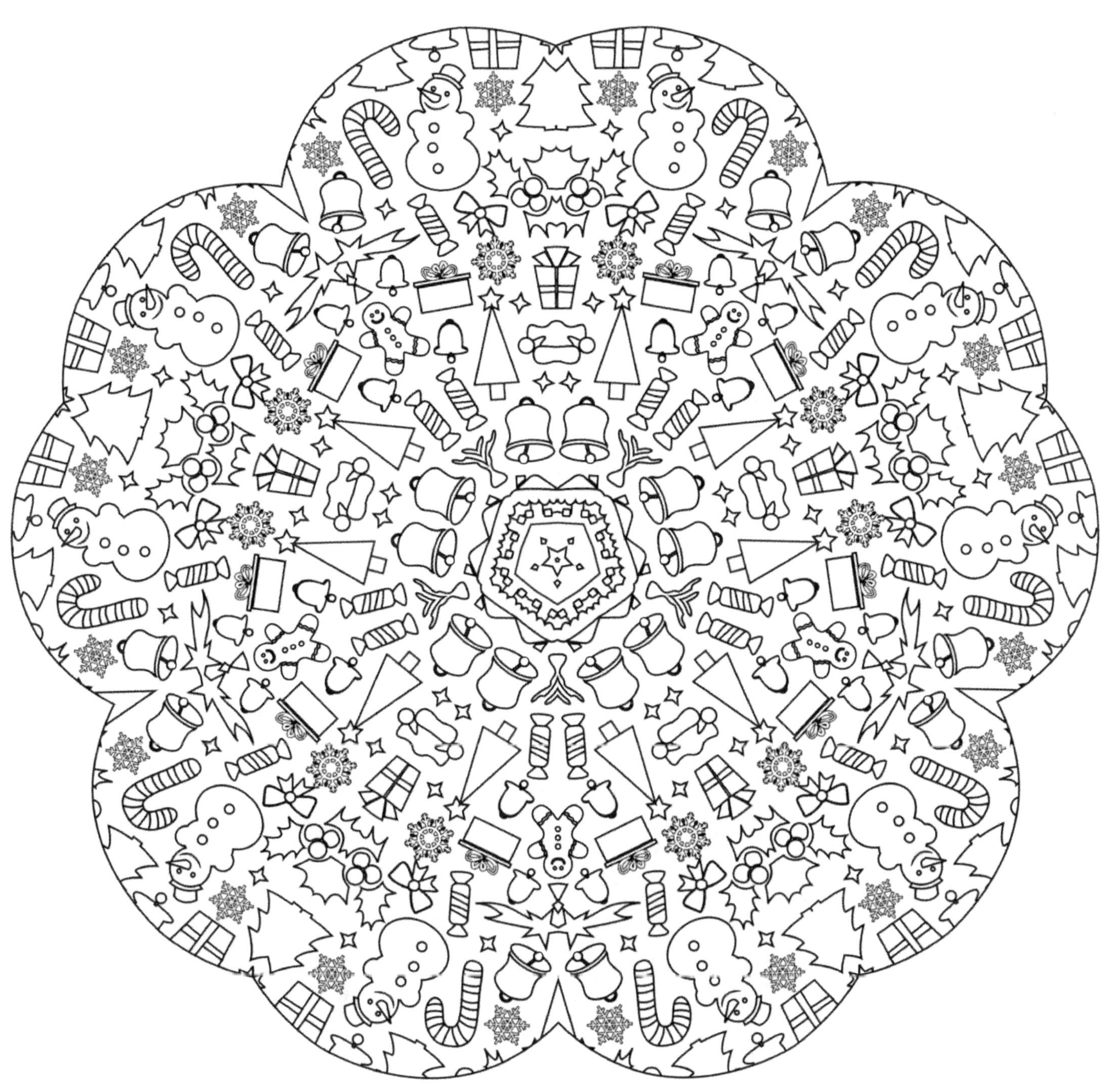

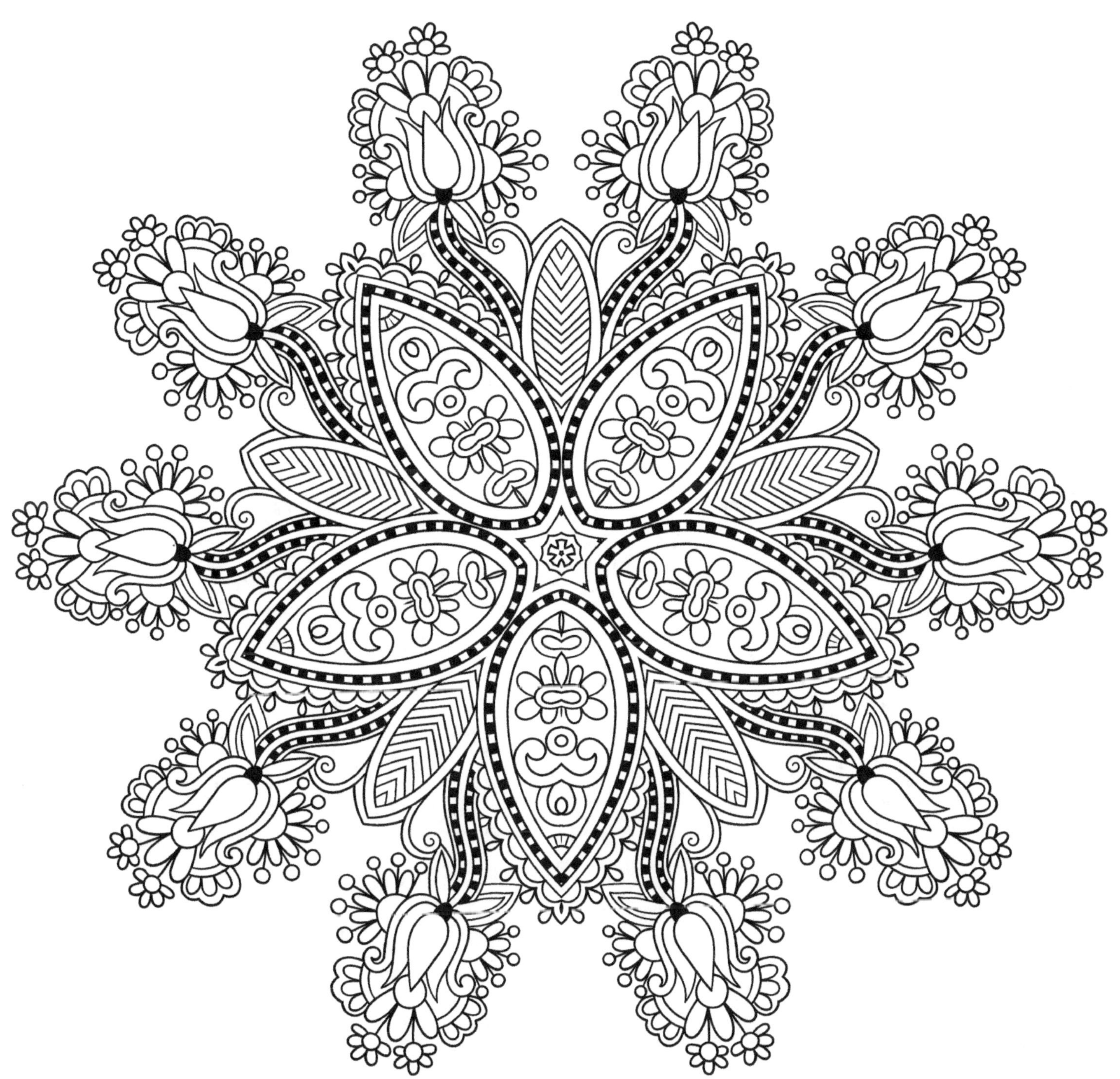

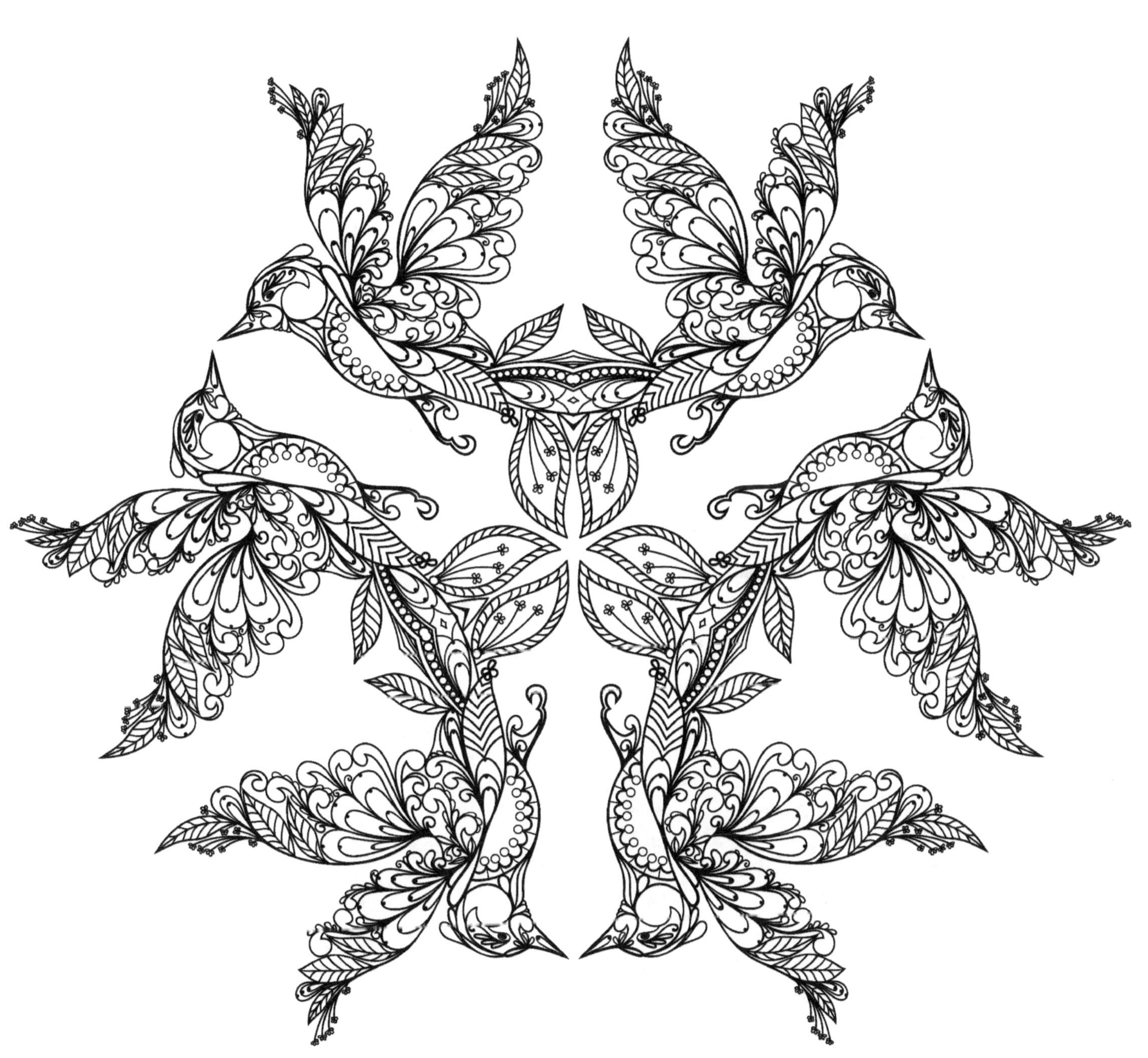

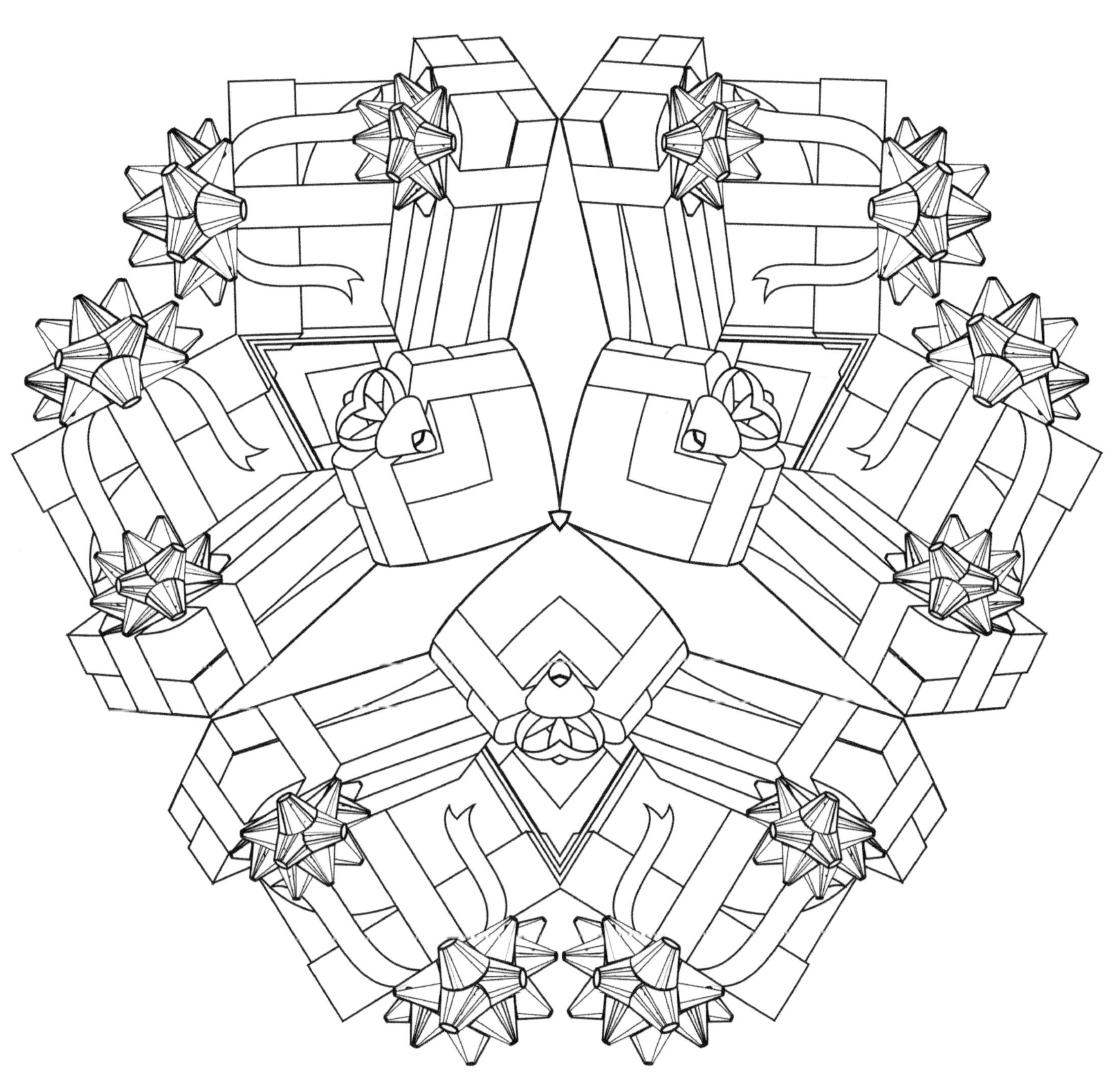

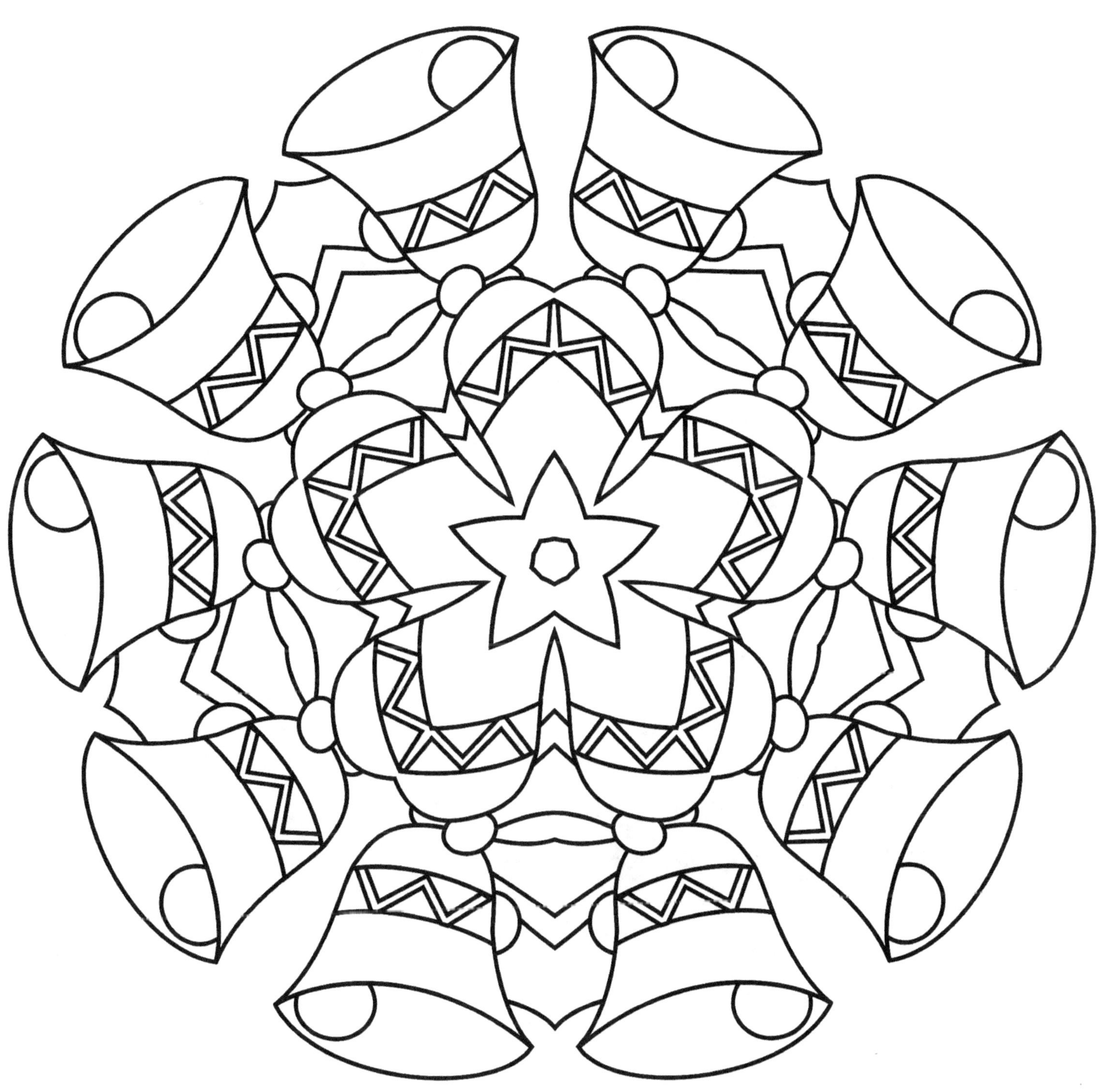

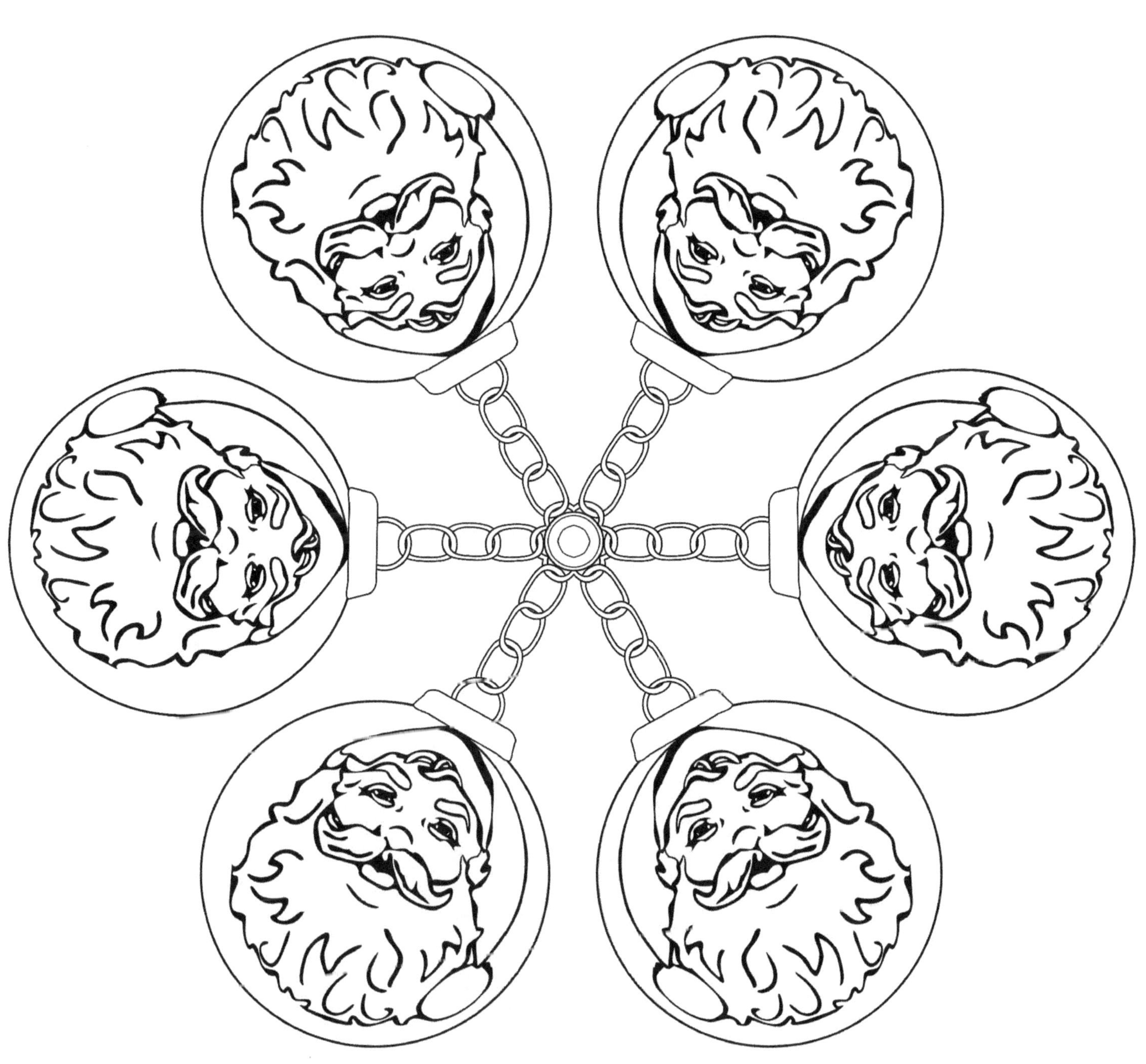

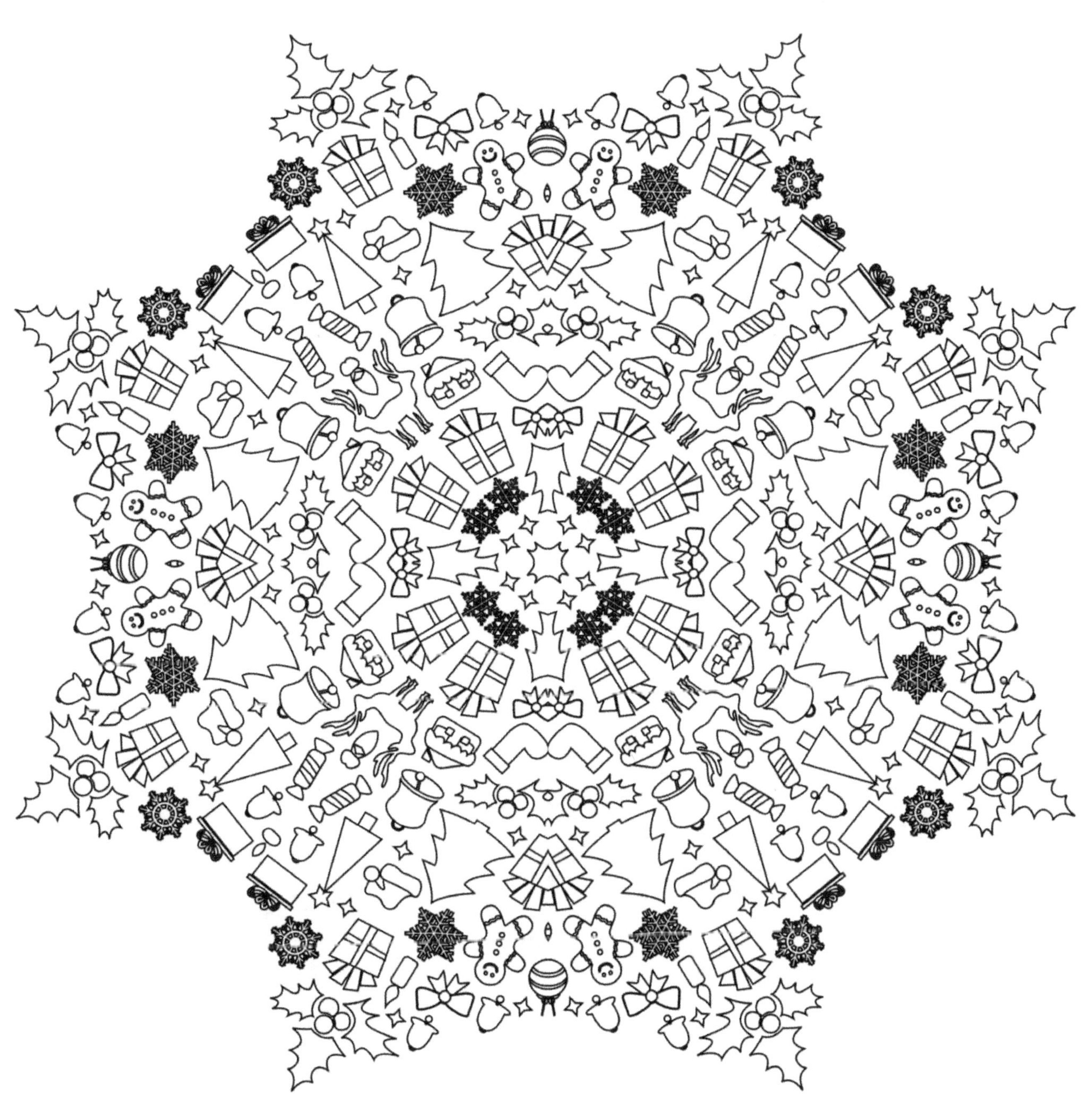

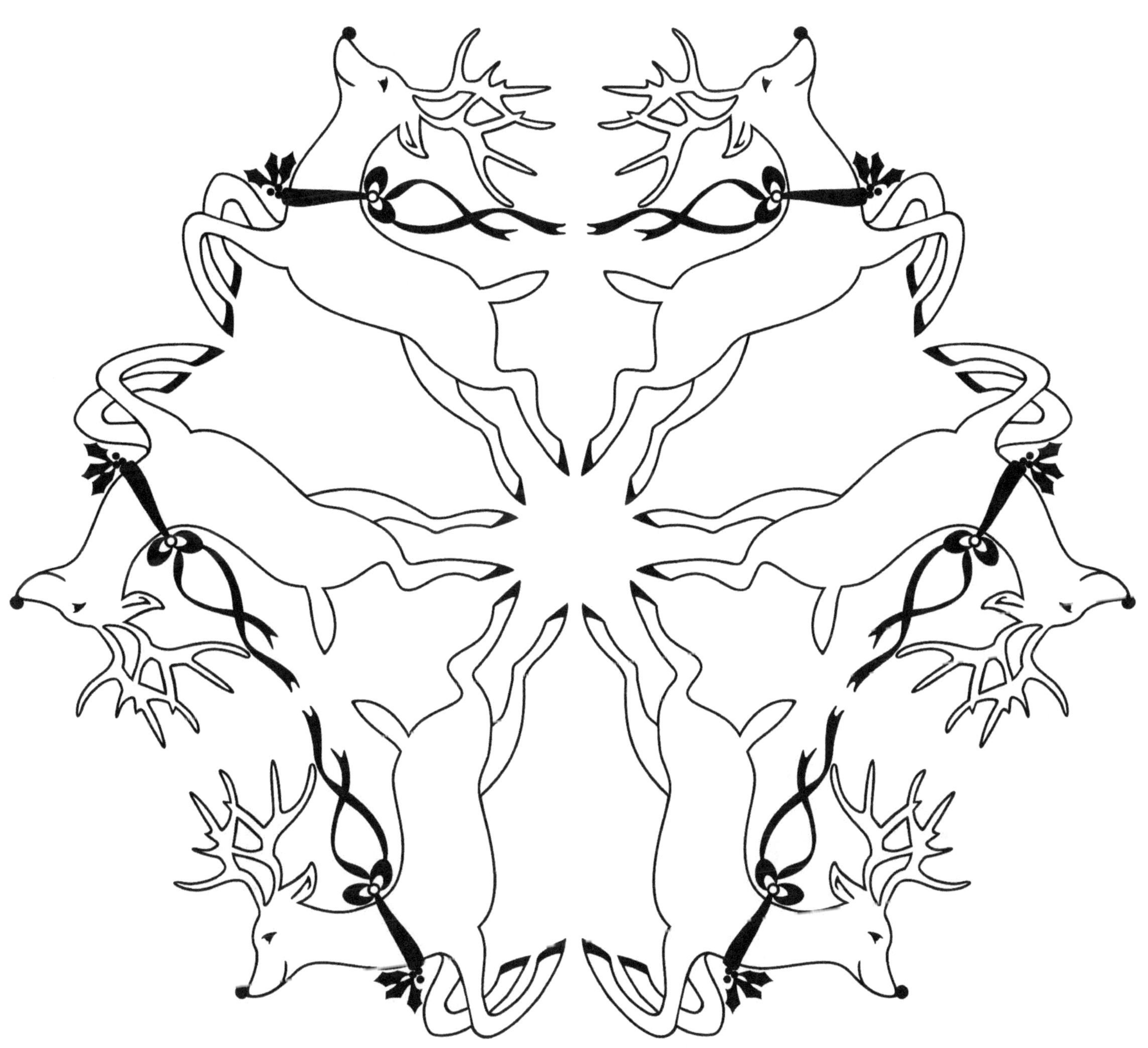

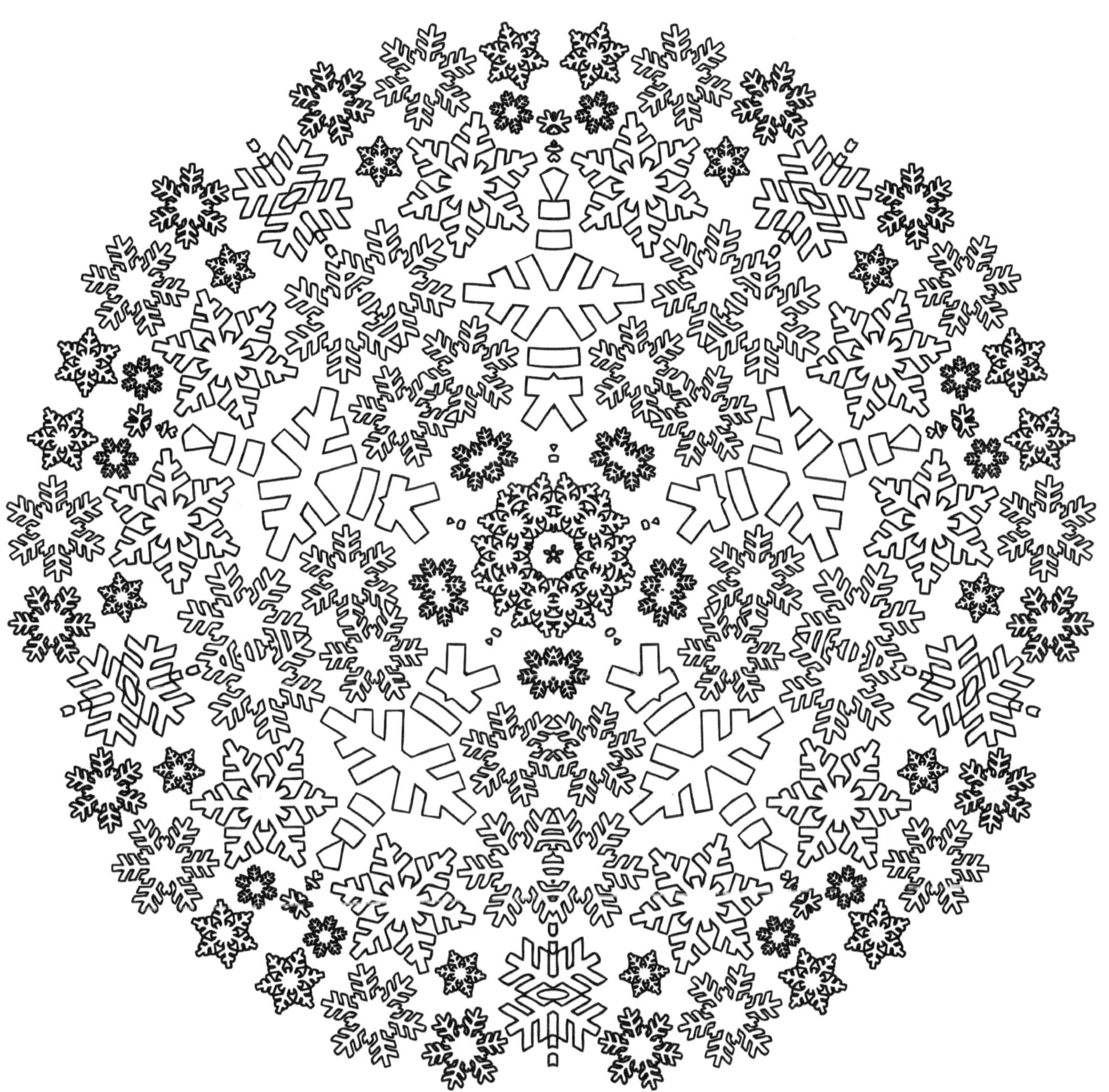

Also available from My Masterpiece®

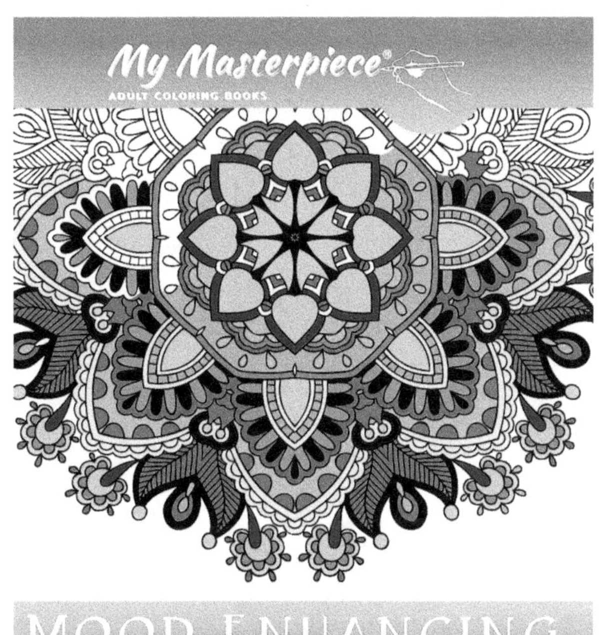

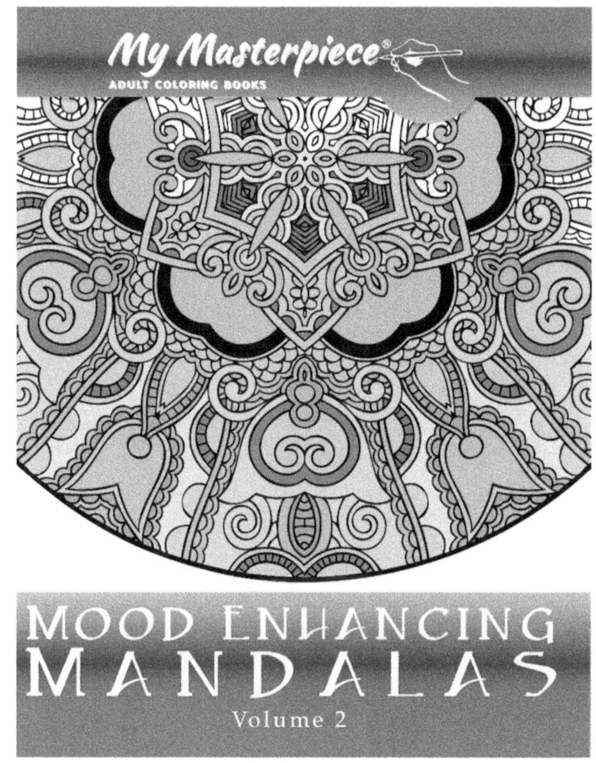

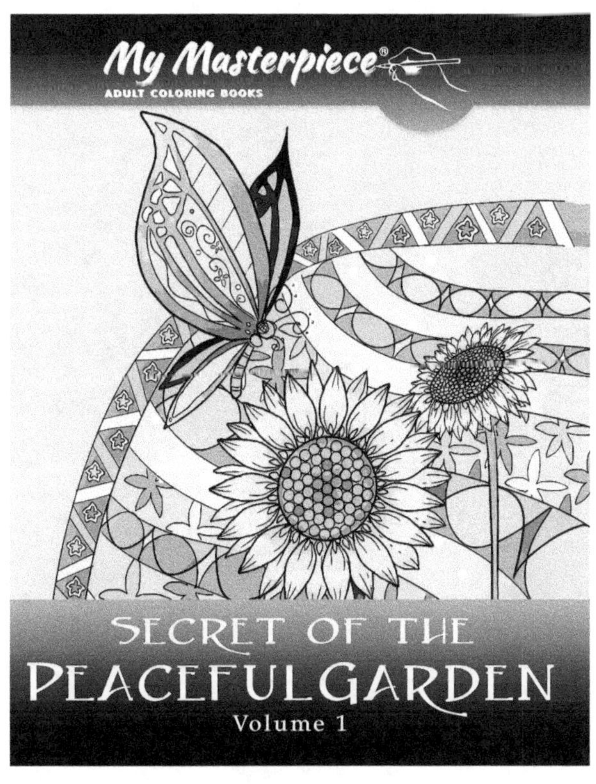

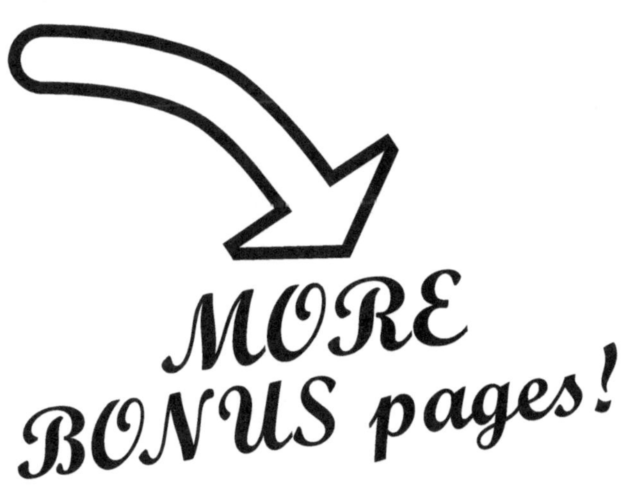

www.mymasterpiececoloring.com

More Bonus Pages

Enjoy the next few pages, where you can try out sample pages from some of our other popular coloring books!

Visit www.MyMasterpieceColoring.com for more!

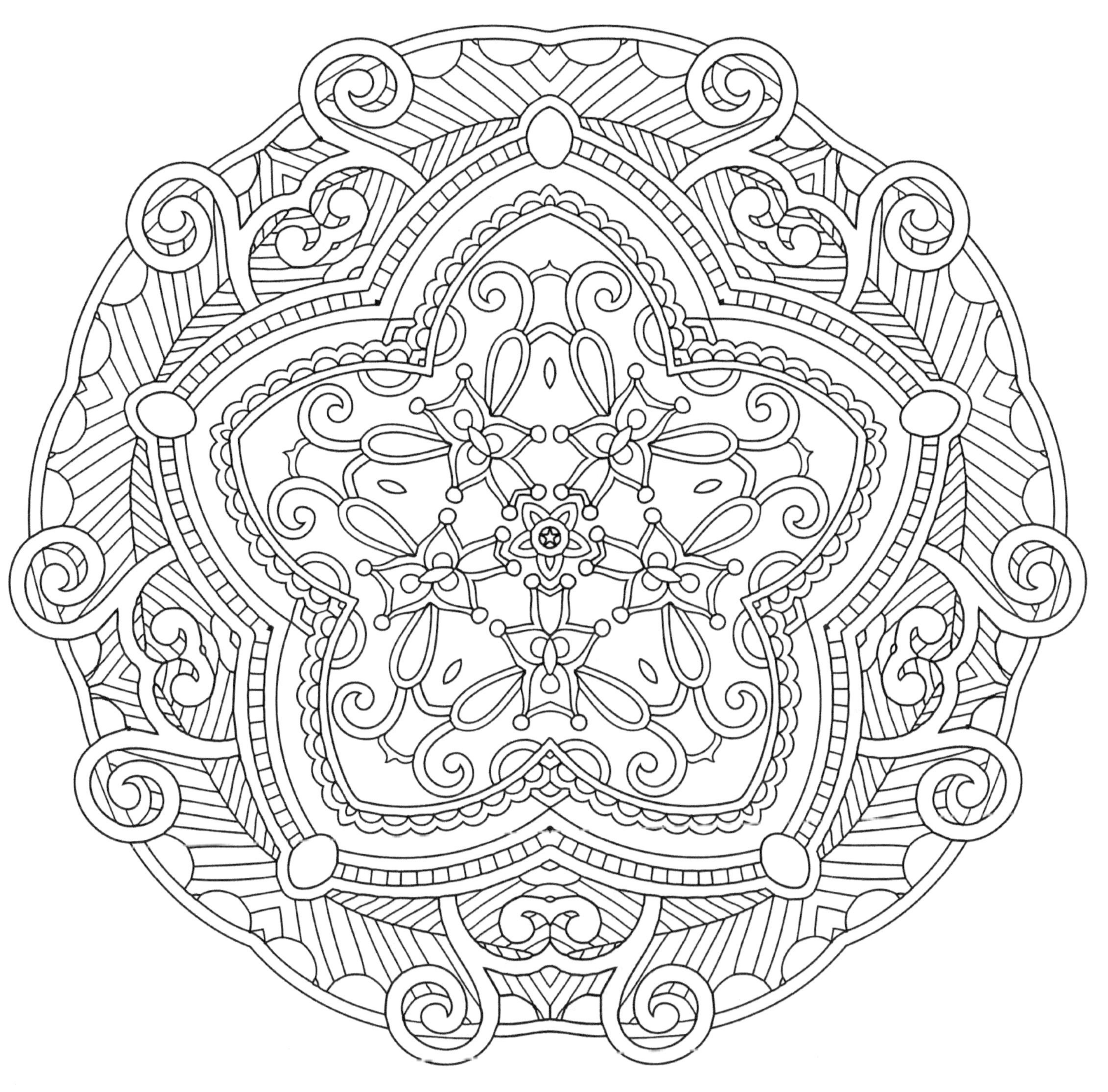

MOOD ENHANCING MANDALAS

VOLUME 1

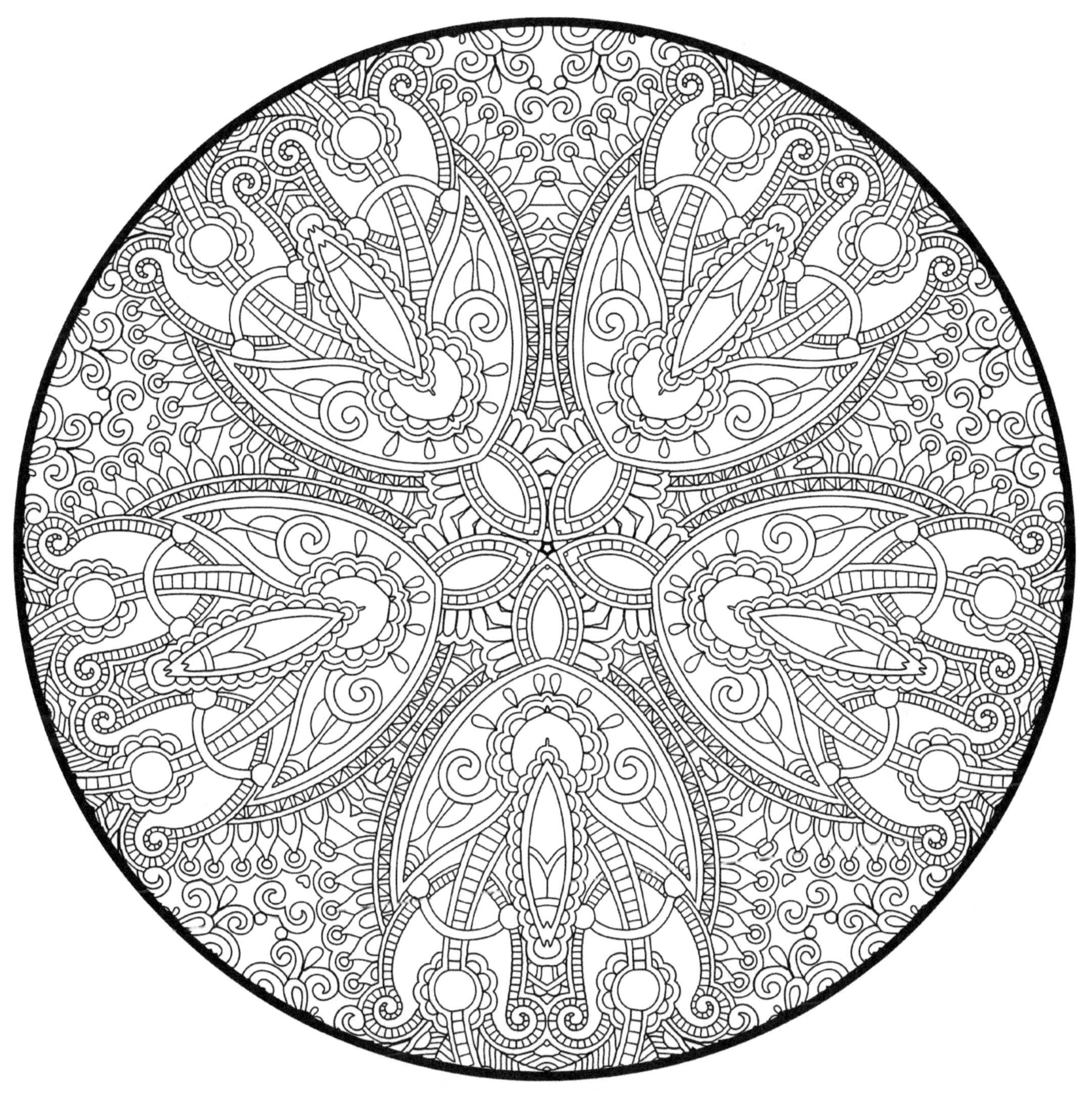

MOOD ENHANCING MANDALAS

VOLUME 2

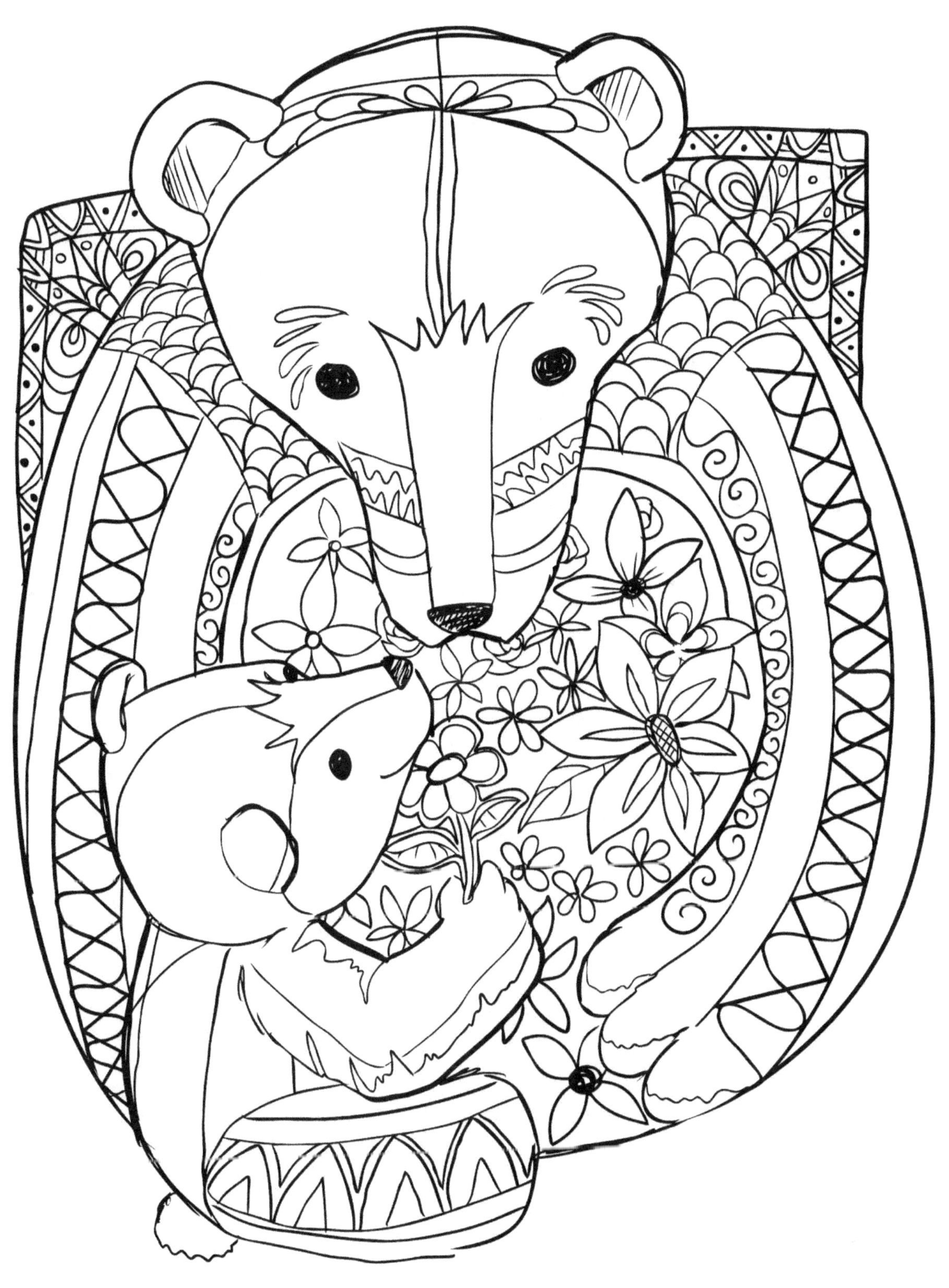

Secret of the Peaceful Garden

Share Your Masterpiece!

Post your colored pages with the hashtag: #MyMasterpieceContest on Instagram, Facebook, Twitter, and Pinterest so we can show off your artistic flair.

Visit www.MyMasterpieceColoring.com to see all the ways you can enter to win great prizes in our monthly Giveaways!

Go To: www.MyMasterpieceColoring.com

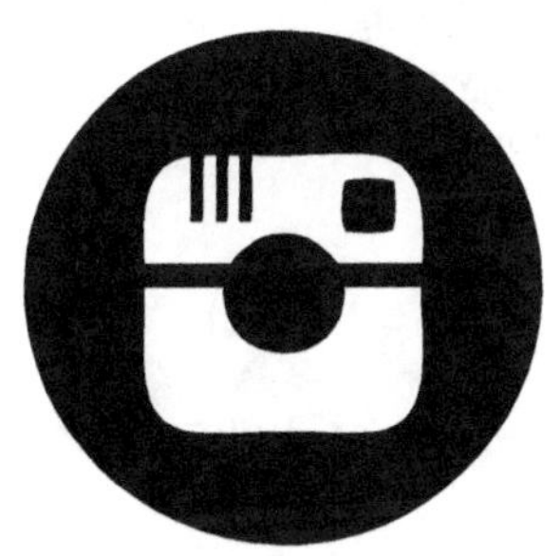

Follow us on Instagram:
www.Instagram.com/MyMasterpieceColoring

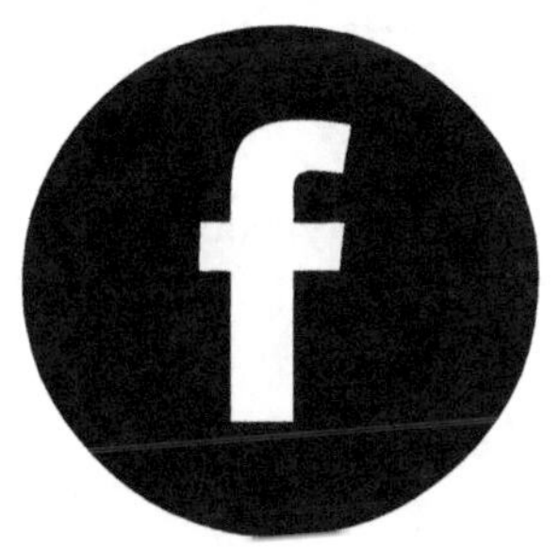

Follow us on Facebook:
www.Facebook.com/MyMasterpieceColoring

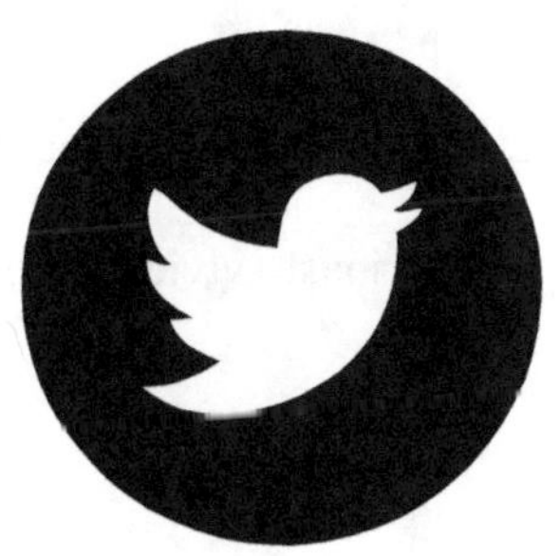

Follow us on Twitter:
www.Twitter.com/MyMasterpieceCo

Follow us on Pinterest:
www.Pinterest.com/MyMasterpieces

Popular Adult Christmas Coloring Books:

A Christmas Carol: A Coloring Classic by Charles Dickens, Kate Ware, and Vladimir Aleksic
A Very Blessed Christmas Coloring Book by Robin Mead
Adult Coloring Book: Christmas Wish: The Perfect Christmas Coloring Book Gift of Love, Blessings, Relaxation and Stress Relief â€“ Christmas Coloring Book by Gina Trowler
Adult Coloring Book: Magic Christmas: for Relaxation Meditation Blessing by Cherina Kohey
Adult coloring books The Special Christmas: Surprisingly wonderful time of this christmas night.Perfect time to enjoy coloring for everyone by Cherina Kohey
Christmas Around the World Coloring Book (Dover Holiday Coloring Book) by Joan O'Brien
Christmas Coloring Book (Coloring Is Fun) by Thaneeya McArdle
Christmas Coloring Book for Adults by Celeste von Albrecht
Christmas Coloring Book for Adults by Happy Coloring
Christmas Coloring Book for Adults Fantastically Festive Patterns and Designs for Christmas Sparkle: Coloring Books Designed for Artists, Adults, Teens and Older Children by Grace Sure
Christmas Coloring Book for Adults: Christmas Trees, Winter Scenes and Christmas Holiday Coloring Book by Ciparum, LLC
Christmas Coloring Book: A Holiday Coloring Book for Adults by Coloring Pages for Adults, Dylanna Press
Christmas Coloring Book: A Stress Management Coloring Book For Adults by Marti Jo's Coloring
Christmas Designs Adult Coloring Book (31 stress-relieving designs) by Peter Pauper Press
Christmas Magic: Fabulous Festive Designs to Color by ArsEdition
Christmas to Color by Mary Tanana
Christmas Treats: A Holiday Coloring Book (Coloring Journeys) by Catherine M. Benante
Color Christmas Coloring Book: Perfectly Portable Pages (On-The-Go Coloring Book) by Thaneeya McArdle
Creative Haven An Old-Fashioned Christmas Coloring Book (Adult Coloring) by Ted Menten
Creative Haven Christmas Mandalas Coloring Book by Marty Noble
Creative Haven Christmas Trees Coloring Book (Adult Coloring) by Barbara Lanza
Creative Haven ChristmasScapes Coloring Book (Adult Coloring) by Jessica Mazurkiewicz
Creative Haven Merry Christmas Designs Coloring Book by Suzanne Anoushian
Creative Haven Snowflake Mandalas Coloring Book (Adult Coloring) by Marty Noble
Creative Haven Ugly Holiday Sweaters Coloring Book (Adult Coloring) by Ellen Christiansen Kraft
Creative Haven Vintage Christmas Greetings Coloring Book (Creative Haven Coloring Books) by Marty Noble
Creative Haven Winter Scenes Coloring Book (Adult Coloring) by Marty Noble
Creative Haven Winter Wonderland Coloring Book (Adult Coloring) by Teresa Goodridge
Creative Haven WinterScapes Coloring Book (Adult Coloring) by Jessica Mazurkiewicz
Festive Christmas: Colouring Book by De-ann Black
Holiday Spirit: Grayscale Coloring Book for Adults by Majestic Coloring
Home for the Holidays: A Hand-Crafted Adult Coloring Book by Galadriel A.L. Thompson
Johanna's Christmas: A Festive Coloring Book for Adults by Johanna Basford
Magical Christmas Adult Coloring Book by Cindy Elsharouni
Mary Engelbreit's Color ME Christmas Coloring Book by Mary Engelbreit
Merry & Bright Holiday Coloring Book by Thaneeya McArdle, Robin Pickens, Angelea Van Dam, Valerie McKeehan, Jenny Newland and William Vanderdasson
Merry Christmas: a beautiful colouring book with Christmas designs on a black background, for gloriously vivid colours by Alexandra Dannenmann
Peace. Joy. Color.: Celebrate the Season with 20 Tear-Out Coloring Cards by Adams Media
Santa's Big Big Book to Color by Golden Books
Santa's Cats: Christmas Adult Coloring Book by Jason Hamilton
Sherri Baldy My Besties Christmas Cottage Coloring Book by Sherri Ann Baldy
Sherri Baldy My-Besties TM Winter Wonderland Filled With Love Coloring Book: Sherri Baldy Christmas Holiday Coloring Book by Sherri Ann Baldy
Sherri Baldy My-Besties Winter Snowmen Coloring Book by Sherri Ann Baldy
Southern Living Christmas at Home: A Lifestyle Coloring Book by The Editors of Southern Living
The Magical Christmas: A Colouring Book (Magical Colouring Books for Adults) by Lizzie Mary Cullen
The Night Before Christmas Coloring Book by Clement Clarke Moore and John O'Brien
Vive Le Color! Christmas (Adult Coloring Book): Color In; De-stress by Abrams Noterie
Winter Magic: Beautiful Holiday Patterns Coloring Book for Adults (Color Magic) by ArsEdition
Wonderful Christmas Coloring Book for Adults by Happy Coloring

Need More Christmas Coloring Books? Try Looking Up These Categories:

adult christmas color books | adult christmas coloring books | adult christmas coloring books 2016 | adult christmas coloring books best sellers | adult christmas coloring books by dover publishing | adult christmas coloring books dover | adult christmas coloring pages | adult christmas colouring books | adult christmas tree coloring book | adult color books christmas | adult coloring books about christmas | adult coloring books christian | adult coloring books christmas | adult coloring books christmas 2017 | adult coloring books christmas religious | adult coloring books christmas scenes | adult coloring books christmas themes | adult coloring books christmas treats | adult coloring books christmas trees | adult coloring books nutcracker | adult coloring books winter | adult coloring books winter scenes | adult coloring books winter wonderland | adult holiday coloring books | adult santa coloring books | adult xmas coloring books | best selling christmas books for adults | best selling christmas books for kids | children's christmas coloring books | christmas adult coloring | christmas adult coloring books | christmas adult coloring books best sellers | christmas adult colouring books | christmas carol coloring book | christmas coloring book for adults | christmas coloring book for kids | christmas coloring book for teens | christmas coloring book johanna basford | christmas coloring book millie marotta | christmas coloring books | christmas coloring books for adults | christmas coloring books for adults a winter scenes coloring book | christmas coloring books for adults relaxation | christmas coloring books for adults vintage | christmas coloring books for children | christmas coloring books for kids | christmas mandala coloring books | christmas nativity coloring books | christmas scenes coloring book | christmas tree coloring book | coloring books christian | coloring books christmas | coloring books for adults christmas | coloring books holidays | coloring books santa | coloring books xmas | elf coloring book | elves coloring book | gingerbread house coloring book | gingerbread man coloring book | grownup coloring books | holiday adult coloring | holiday adult coloring books | holiday adult coloring books best sellers | holiday coloring books for adults | holiday coloring books for adults relaxation | holiday coloring books for kids | merry christmas coloring book | millie marotta christmas | nativity coloring book | nativity coloring books for adults | nutcracker coloring book | poinsettia coloring books | reindeer coloring book | santa clause coloring book | snow globe coloring book | snowman coloring book | snowman coloring books for adults | ugly sweater coloring book | winter coloring books for adults | winter coloring books for kids | winter wonderland coloring book | xmas coloring books

Popular Coloring Pens & Coloring Pencil Sets Available From Amazon

Fiskars Gel Pen 48-Piece Value Set ASIN: B000S161FO
Best Gel Pens - 60 Gel Pen Set with Case - Perfect Art Micron Ink Pen Set ASIN: B00ZGQD4GU
1 X 52 GEL Pens W/comfort Grips & Tin Storage Case ASIN: B004KRNLJ6
Super Doodle Gel Pens - Professional High Quality 36 Piece Set - Smooth Flowing Ink ASIN: B00ZSBLW80
Sakura 38176 10-Piece Gelly Roll Assorted Colors Bold Point Gel Ink Pen Set ASIN: B000GZOCA8
Sargent Art 22-1501 10-Count Glitter Gel Pens ASIN: B005V9V6L2
Crayola 50ct Long Colored Pencils ASIN: B00000J0S3
Sargent Art 22-7251 50-Count Assorted Colored Pencils ASIN: B0027PA1AU
Prismacolor Premier Colored Pencils, 24 Pack by Sanford ASIN: B00006IEEU
Prismacolor Premier Soft Core Colored Pencils by Sanford ASIN: B000E23RSQ
US Art Supply 50 Piece Artist Grade High Quality Colored Pencil Set ASIN: B00Q3HWHX2
Prang Colored Pencil Set, Thick Core ASIN: B002GYFFP8
Pentel Color Pen Set, Set of 36 Assorted Colors (S360-36) ASIN: B001E6F108
AmazaPens Gel Coloring Pens - 40% More Ink Than Other Sets! ASIN: B00ZT641W8
48 Colored Pencils for Secret Garden Adult Coloring Book Professional Colored Drawing Pencil ASIN: B0149QWDO6
Ohuhu 48-color Colored Pencils/ Drawing Pencils for Sketch/Secret Garden Coloring Book ASIN: B00U78NQHO
Darice 80-Piece Deluxe Art Set ASIN: B002NZJ4L6
Art 101 142-Piece Wood Art Set ASIN: B002KW3OQS
Darice 120-Piece Deluxe Art Set ASIN: B002PNV6YE
LolliZ Gel Pens | 96 Gel Pen Set - 2 Packs of 48 pens each ASIN: B00KO8UK80

www.ingramcontent.com/pod-product-compliance
Lightning Source LLC
LaVergne TN
LVHW061251100826
845148LV00008B/1092